MATH

Here's a short note for parents:

We recommend that you work through this book with your child, offering guidance and encouragement along the way.

Find a quiet place to sit, preferably at a table, and encourage your child to hold their pencil correctly.

Try to work at your child's pace and avoid spending too long on any one page or activity.

Most of all, emphasize the fun element of what you are doing and enjoy yourselves. You can add a reward sticker to the bottom of each page as you complete it.

Reward sticker!

AUTUMN PUBLISHING

Count to 100

What numbers are missing from this grid?
Fill in the missing numbers below.

1	2		4	5	6		8	9	10
11		13	14		16	17		19	
21	22	23		25		27	28		30
	32		34		36	37	38	39	40
41		43	44	45			48	49	
51	52		54		56	57	58		60
61	62	63		65	66	67		69	70
71	72	73	74		76		78	79	
81		83		85		87	88	89	90
	92		94	95	96	97		99	

Reward
sticker!

2

Count in 2s

Help the frog get to her lily pad by writing in the missing numbers in the sequence.

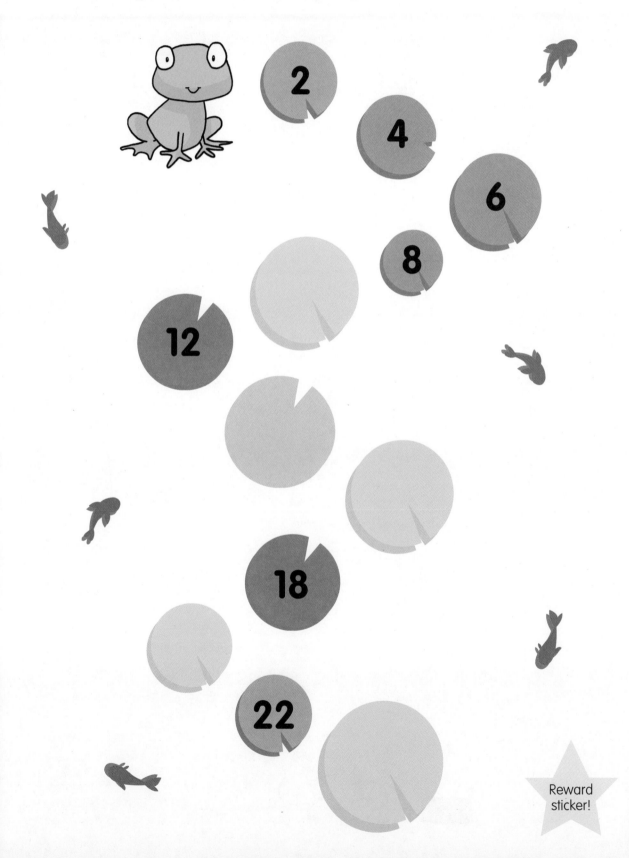

2

4

6

8

12

18

22

Reward sticker!

One more, one less

Practice adding and subtracting by 1 in the equations below. Write the answers in the boxes.

7 + 1 = 8   2 − 1 = 1

4 + 1 =   8 − 1 =

8 + 1 =   5 − 1 =

3 + 1 =   3 − 1 =

6 + 1 =   7 − 1 =

Reward sticker!

Grouping

Draw circles to put the bees into groups of 3.

How many groups are there?

How many bees are there all together?

Draw circles to put these candies into groups of 4.

How many groups are there?

How many candies are there all together?

Adding up

Do the additions below, writing the answers in the boxes.

1 + 2 = ☐   4 + 8 = ☐

6 + 5 = ☐   2 + 10 = ☐

8 + 1 = ☐   3 + 5 = ☐

3 + 3 = ☐   9 + 4 = ☐

6 + 8 = ☐   8 + 8 = ☐

10 + 10 = ☐   9 + 9 = ☐

Reward sticker!

Making 10

Put a ✓ after each question that makes 10. Put a **X** after the ones that don't.

5 + 5 7 + 4

2 + 9  1 + 9

8 + 2 2 + 8

3 + 7  7 + 3

6 + 7 6 + 4

9 + 1  3 + 8

4 + 6 7 + 7

Reward sticker!

Taking away

Do the subtractions below, writing the answers in the boxes.

5 – 2 = ☐   7 – 2 = ☐

6 – 2 = ☐   13 – 12 = ☐

12 – 6 = ☐   20 – 11 = ☐

7 – 6 = ☐   18 – 9 = ☐

3 – 2 = ☐   16 – 14 = ☐

8 – 5 = ☐   4 – 2 = ☐

Making 20

Color the diamond after every question that makes 20.

12 + 8   12 + 8

13 + 7   19 + 1

20 - 2   10 + 10

24 - 4   11 + 8

15 + 6   14 + 8

16 + 4   26 + 6

25 - 5   15 + 5

Reward sticker!

Count in 5s and 10s

Fill in the numbers to help each frog follow its path to the other side of the lily pond.

5

10

15

20

30

35

45

60

Reward sticker!

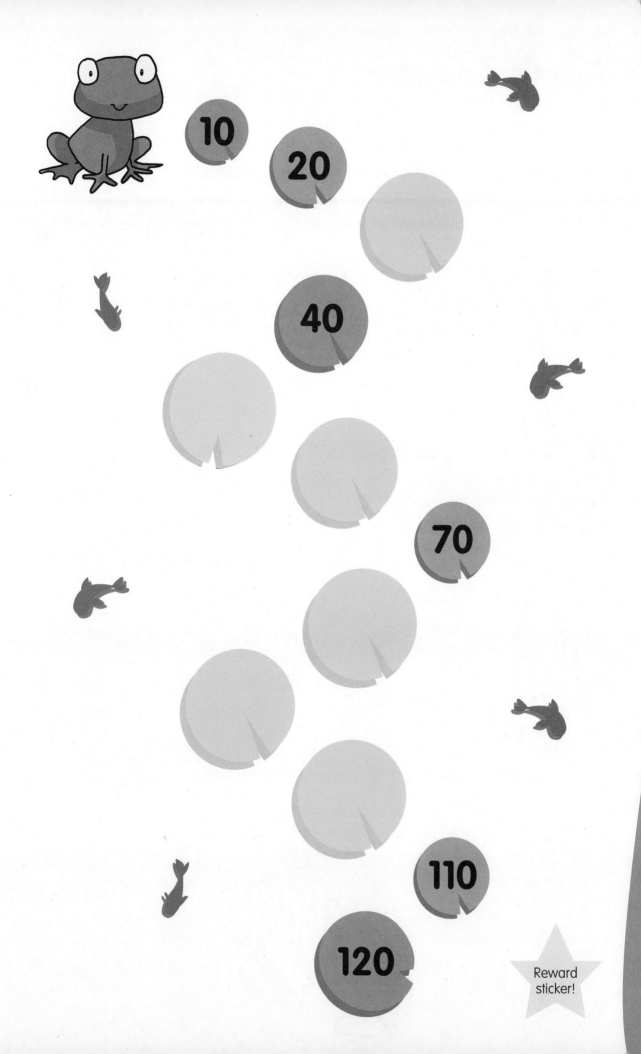

10

20

40

70

110

120

Missing numbers

Fill in the missing numbers below to solve these out-of-this-world addition and subtraction problems.

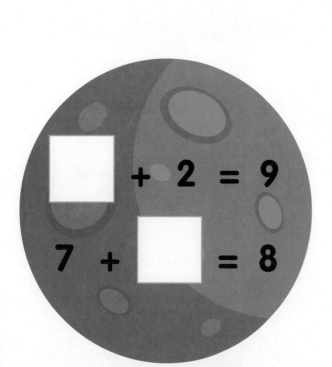

☐ + 2 = 9

7 + ☐ = 8

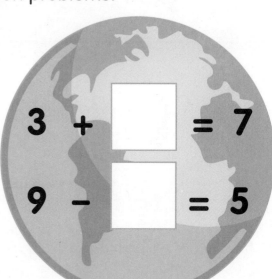

3 + ☐ = 7

9 − ☐ = 5

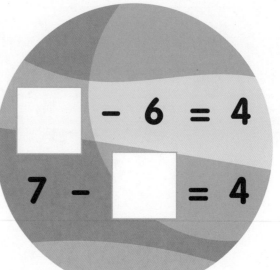

☐ − 6 = 4

7 − ☐ = 4

9 − ☐ = 4

☐ + 3 = 8

$\boxed{}$ + 12 = 19

7 + $\boxed{}$ = 15

3 + $\boxed{}$ = 20

8 + $\boxed{}$ = 17

$\boxed{}$ − 6 = 11

16 − $\boxed{}$ = 11

19 − $\boxed{}$ = 14

$\boxed{}$ + 3 = 18

Reward sticker!

Multiplying by 2

Complete the 2 times multiplication questions below.
Write the answers in the boxes.

1 x 2 = ☐

7 x 2 = ☐

2 x 2 = ☐

8 x 2 = ☐

3 x 2 = ☐

9 x 2 = ☐

4 x 2 = ☐

10 x 2 = ☐

5 x 2 = ☐

11 x 2 = ☐

6 x 2 = ☐

12 x 2 = ☐

Reward
sticker!

Number patterns x2

Color each square that shows an answer from the last page.
This is the pattern of your 2 times table! Can you carry on
the pattern all the way to 100?

1	2	3	4	5	6	7	8	9	10
11	12	13	14	15	16	17	18	19	20
21	22	23	24	25	26	27	28	29	30
31	32	33	34	35	36	37	38	39	40
41	42	43	44	45	46	47	48	49	50
51	52	53	54	55	56	57	58	59	60
61	62	63	64	65	66	67	68	69	70
71	72	73	74	75	76	77	78	79	80
81	82	83	84	85	86	87	88	89	90
91	92	93	94	95	96	97	98	99	100

Reward
sticker!

Multiplying by 5

Complete the 5 times multiplication problems below.
Write the answers in the boxes.

1 x 5 = ☐   7 x 5 = ☐

2 x 5 = ☐   8 x 5 = ☐

3 x 5 = ☐   9 x 5 = ☐

4 x 5 = ☐   10 x 5 = ☐

5 x 5 = ☐   11 x 5 = ☐

6 x 5 = ☐   12 x 5 = ☐

Reward
sticker!

16

Number patterns x5

Color each square that shows an answer from the last page. This is the pattern of your 5 times table! Can you carry on the pattern all the way to 100?

1	2	3	4	5	6	7	8	9	10
11	12	13	14	15	16	17	18	19	20
21	22	23	24	25	26	27	28	29	30
31	32	33	34	35	36	37	38	39	40
41	42	43	44	45	46	47	48	49	50
51	52	53	54	55	56	57	58	59	60
61	62	63	64	65	66	67	68	69	70
71	72	73	74	75	76	77	78	79	80
81	82	83	84	85	86	87	88	89	90
91	92	93	94	95	96	97	98	99	100

Reward sticker!

Multiplying by 10

Complete the 10 times multiplication problems below.
Write the answers in the boxes.

1 x 10 =

7 x 10 =

2 x 10 =

8 x 10 =

3 x 10 =

9 x 10 =

4 x 10 =

10 x 10 =

5 x 10 =

11 x 10 =

6 x 10 =

12 x 10 =

Reward
sticker!

Number patterns x10

Color each square that shows an answer from the last page.
This is the pattern of your 10 times table! How is the pattern
different to the 2 times and 5 times tables?

1	2	3	4	5	6	7	8	9	10
11	12	13	14	15	16	17	18	19	20
21	22	23	24	25	26	27	28	29	30
31	32	33	34	35	36	37	38	39	40
41	42	43	44	45	46	47	48	49	50
51	52	53	54	55	56	57	58	59	60
61	62	63	64	65	66	67	68	69	70
71	72	73	74	75	76	77	78	79	80
81	82	83	84	85	86	87	88	89	90
91	92	93	94	95	96	97	98	99	100

Reward
sticker!

Double bubble

Double the numbers in each of the bubbles below.
Hint: **double 4** is the same as **4 + 4**.

Double 4

Double 9

Double 7

Double 6

Double 5

Double 8

2D shapes

A 2D (two-dimensional) shape is a shape that has length and width, but no height. This means that it is flat.

Count all of the **squares** below. How many are there all together? Write your answer in the box.

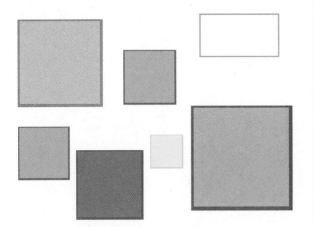

Count all of the **rectangles** below. How many are there all together? Write your answer in the box.

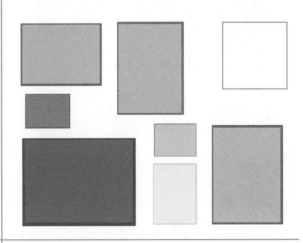

Count all of the **circles** below. How many are there all together? Write your answer in the box.

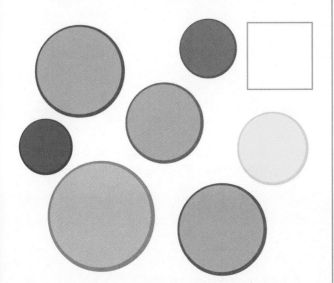

Count all of the **triangles** below. How many are there all together? Write your answer in the box.

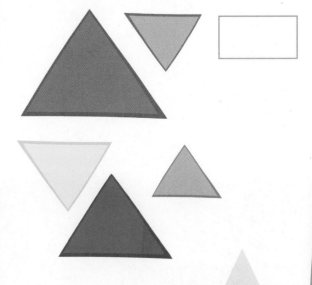

Reward sticker!

Halves

Shade in **half** of each of the shapes below.
The first shape has been done for you.

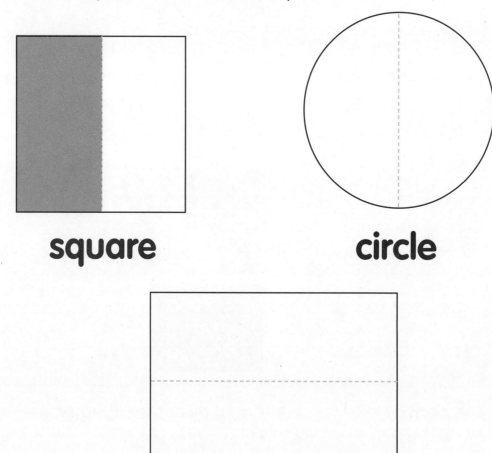

square

circle

rectangle

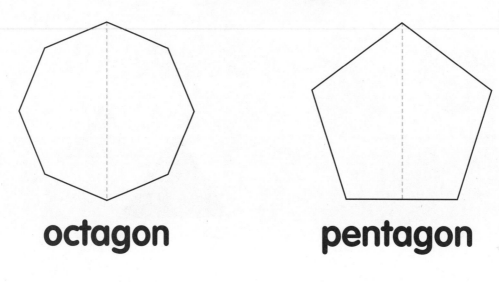

octagon

pentagon

Reward
sticker!

Draw a ring around **half** of the objects for each of the below.
Then read the questions and write your answers in the boxes.

a.

What is half of 4?

b.

What is half of 6?

c.

What is half of 12?

Reward
sticker!

Quarters

Shade in a **quarter** of each of the shapes below.
The first shape has been done for you.

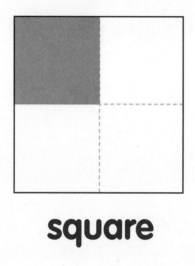

square

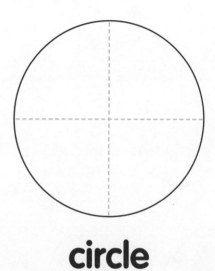

circle

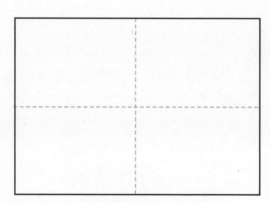

rectangle

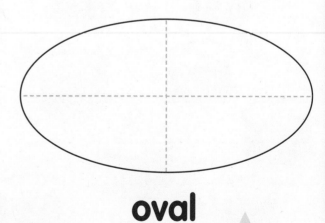

oval

Reward
sticker!

24

Draw a ring around a **quarter** of the objects for each of the below. Then read the questions and write your answers in the boxes.

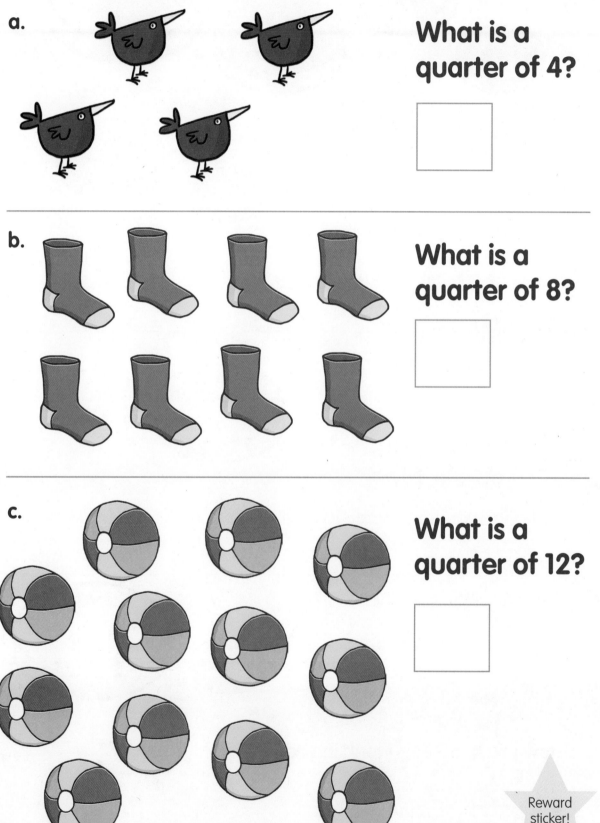

a.

What is a quarter of 4?

b.

What is a quarter of 8?

c.

What is a quarter of 12?

Reward sticker!

Coins

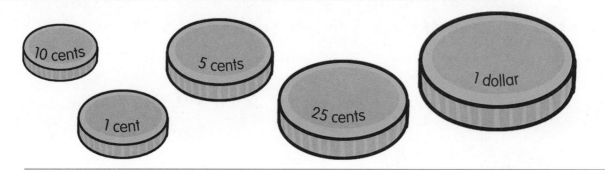

a. What two coins are these?

____ and ____

How much are they worth in total?

b. What two coins are these?

____ and ____

How much are they worth in total?

c. What two coins are these?

____ and ____

How much are they worth in total?

3D shapes

A 3D (three-dimensional) shape is a shape that has length, width, and height. Take a look at the 3D shapes below.

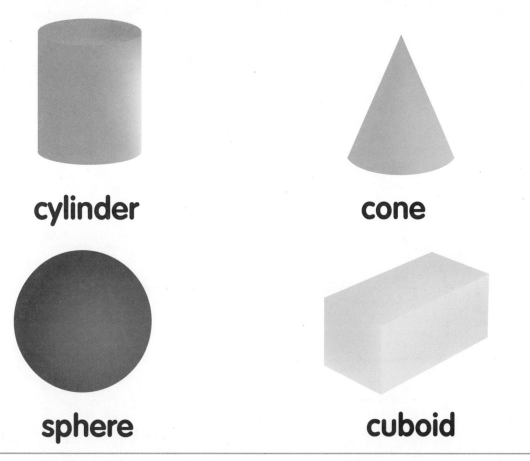

cylinder

cone

sphere

cuboid

This is a face

There are 6 faces on a cube.

How many faces does a cuboid have?

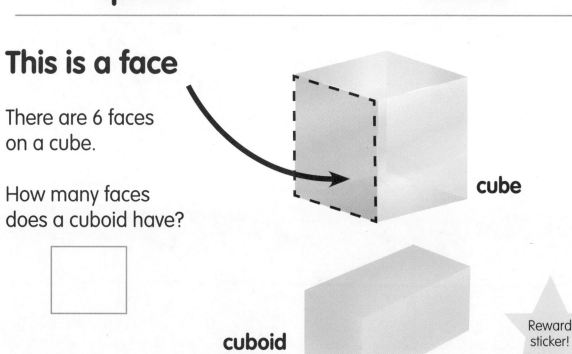

cube

cuboid

Reward sticker!

Color by shapes

Follow the code to color this picture.
Choose your own colors where there are no code symbols.

triangle

light blue

circle

light green

square

dark blue

star

dark green

Reward sticker!

28

Number patterns

Look carefully at these number cards.

Then, use the cards to complete the number patterns below.

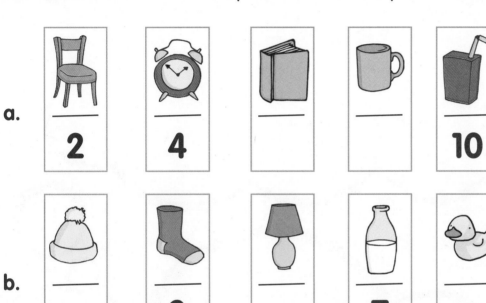

a.

2   4   ___   ___   10

b.

___   3   ___   7   ___

c.

___   ___   3   ___   1

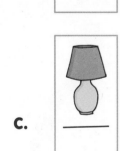

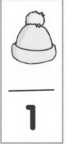

d.

___   ___   8   7   ___

Reward
sticker!

29

Mental math

Answer the sums below in your head.
Write the answers in the boxes.

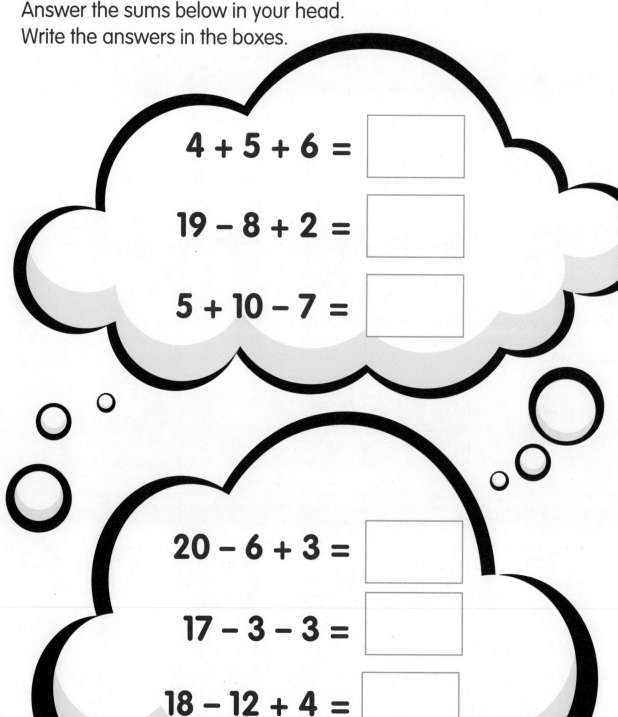

$4 + 5 + 6 = $

$19 - 8 + 2 = $

$5 + 10 - 7 = $

$20 - 6 + 3 = $

$17 - 3 - 3 = $

$18 - 12 + 4 = $

Reward sticker!

Answers:

Page 2: Count to 100

1	2	**3**	4	5	6	**7**	8	9	10
11	**12**	13	14	**15**	16	17	**18**	19	**20**
21	22	23	**24**	25	**26**	27	28	**29**	30
31	32	**33**	34	**35**	36	37	38	39	40
41	**42**	43	44	45	**46**	**47**	48	49	**50**
51	52	**53**	54	**55**	56	57	58	**59**	60
61	62	63	**64**	65	66	67	**68**	69	70
71	72	73	74	**75**	76	**77**	78	79	**80**
81	**82**	83	**84**	85	**86**	87	88	89	90
91	92	**93**	94	95	96	97	**98**	99	**100**

Page 3: Count in 2s

2, 4, 6, 8, **10**, 12, **14**, **16**, 18, **20**, 22, **24**

Page 4: One more, one less

4 + 1 = **5**	8 − 1 = **7**
8 + 1 = **9**	5 − 1 = **4**
3 + 1 = **4**	3 − 1 = **2**
6 + 1 = **7**	7 − 1 = **6**

Page 5: Grouping

5 groups of bees, 15 bees altogether
3 groups of sweets, 12 sweets altogether

Page 6: Adding up

1 + 2 = **3**	4 + 8 = **12**
6 + 5 = **11**	2 + 10 = **12**
8 + 1 = **9**	3 + 5 = **8**
3 + 3 = **6**	9 + 4 = **13**
6 + 8 = **14**	8 + 8 = **16**
10 + 10 = **20**	9 + 9 = **18**

Page 7: Making 10

5 + 5 = 10	7 + 4 = 11
2 + 9 = 11	1 + 9 = 10
8 + 2 = 10	2 + 8 = 10
3 + 7 = 10	7 + 3 = 10
6 + 7 = 13	6 + 4 = 10
9 + 1 = 10	3 + 8 = 11
4 + 6 = 10	7 + 7 = 14

Page 8: Taking away

5 − 2 = **3**	7 − 2 = **5**
6 − 2 = **4**	13 − 12 = **1**
12 − 6 = **6**	20 − 11 = **9**
7 − 6 = **1**	18 − 9 = **9**
3 − 2 = **1**	16 − 14 = **2**
8 − 5 = **3**	4 − 2 = **2**

Page 9: Making 20

12 + 8	◆	12 + 8	◆
13 + 7	◆	19 + 1	◆
20 − 2	◇	10 + 10	◆
24 − 4	◆	11 + 8	◇
15 + 6	◇	14 + 8	◇
16 + 4	◆	26 + 6	◇
25 − 5	◆	15 + 5	◆

Pages 10-11: Count in 5s and 10s

5, 10, 15, 20, **25**, 30, 35, **40**, 45, **50**, **55**, 60
10, 20, **30**, 40, **50**, **60**, 70, **80**, **90**, **100**, 110, 120

Pages 12-13: Missing numbers

7 + 2 = 9	7 + **1** = 8
3 + **4** = 7	9 − **4** = 5
9 − **5** = 4	**5** + 3 = 8
10 − 6 = 4	7 − **3** = 4
7 + 12 = 19	7 + **8** = 15
3 + **17** = 20	8 + **9** = 17
17 − 6 = 11	16 − **5** = 11
19 − **5** = 14	**15** + 3 = 18

Page 14: Multiplying by 2

1 x 2 = **2**	7 x 2 = **14**
2 x 2 = **4**	8 x 2 = **16**
3 x 2 = **6**	9 x 2 = **18**
4 x 2 = **8**	10 x 2 = **20**
5 x 2 = **10**	11 x 2 = **22**
6 x 2 = **12**	12 x 2 = **24**

Answers:

Page 15: Number patterns x2

1	2	3	4	5	6	7	8	9	10
11	12	13	14	15	16	17	18	19	20
21	22	23	24	25	26	27	28	29	30
31	32	33	34	35	36	37	38	39	40
41	42	43	44	45	46	47	48	49	50
51	52	53	54	55	56	57	58	59	60
61	62	63	64	65	66	67	68	69	70
71	72	73	74	75	76	77	78	79	80
81	82	83	84	85	86	87	88	89	90
91	92	93	94	95	96	97	98	99	100

Page 16: Multiplying by 5

$1 \times 5 = \mathbf{5}$ $7 \times 5 = \mathbf{35}$

$2 \times 5 = \mathbf{10}$ $8 \times 5 = \mathbf{40}$

$3 \times 5 = \mathbf{15}$ $9 \times 5 = \mathbf{45}$

$4 \times 5 = \mathbf{20}$ $10 \times 5 = \mathbf{50}$

$5 \times 5 = \mathbf{25}$ $11 \times 5 = \mathbf{55}$

$6 \times 5 = \mathbf{30}$ $12 \times 5 = \mathbf{60}$

Page 17: Number patterns x5

1	2	3	4	5	6	7	8	9	10
11	12	13	14	15	16	17	18	19	20
21	22	23	24	25	26	27	28	29	30
31	32	33	34	35	36	37	38	39	40
41	42	43	44	45	46	47	48	49	50
51	52	53	54	55	56	57	58	59	60
61	62	63	64	65	66	67	68	69	70
71	72	73	74	75	76	77	78	79	80
81	82	83	84	85	86	87	88	89	90
91	92	93	94	95	96	97	98	99	100

Page 18: Multiplying by 10

$1 \times 10 = \mathbf{10}$ $7 \times 10 = \mathbf{70}$

$2 \times 10 = \mathbf{20}$ $8 \times 10 = \mathbf{80}$

$3 \times 10 = \mathbf{30}$ $9 \times 10 = \mathbf{90}$

$4 \times 10 = \mathbf{40}$ $10 \times 10 = \mathbf{100}$

$5 \times 10 = \mathbf{50}$ $11 \times 10 = \mathbf{110}$

$6 \times 10 = \mathbf{60}$ $12 \times 10 = \mathbf{120}$

Page 19: Number patterns x10

1	2	3	4	5	6	7	8	9	10
11	12	13	14	15	16	17	18	19	20
21	22	23	24	25	26	27	28	29	30
31	32	33	34	35	36	37	38	39	40
41	42	43	44	45	46	47	48	49	50
51	52	53	54	55	56	57	58	59	60
61	62	63	64	65	66	67	68	69	70
71	72	73	74	75	76	77	78	79	80
81	82	83	84	85	86	87	88	89	90
91	92	93	94	95	96	97	98	99	100

Page 20: Double bubble

Double 4 = **8**

Double 9 = **18**

Double 7 = **14**

Double 6 = **12**

Double 5 = **10**

Double 8 = **16**

Page 21: 2D shapes

6 squares 7 rectangles

7 circles 5 triangles

Pages 22-23: Halves

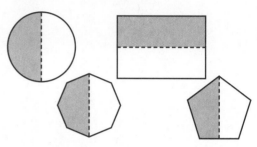

<u>a.</u> 2 <u>b.</u> 3 <u>c.</u> 6

Pages 24-25: Quarters

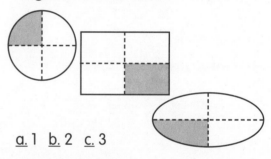

<u>a.</u> 1 <u>b.</u> 2 <u>c.</u> 3

Page 26: Coins

<u>a.</u> 10¢ + 1¢ = 11¢

<u>b.</u> 25¢ + 5¢ = 30¢

<u>c.</u> 10¢ + $1 = $1.10

Page 27: 3D shapes

The cuboid has 6 faces.

Page 29: Number patterns

<u>a.</u> 2, 4, **6**, **8**,10

<u>b.</u> **1**, 3, **5**, 7, **9**

<u>c.</u> **5**, 4, 3, **2**, 1

<u>d.</u> **10**, **9**, 8, 7, **6**

Page 30: Mental math

4 + 5 + 6 = **15**

19 − 8 + 2 = **13**

5 + 10 − 7 = **8**

20 − 6 + 3 = **17**

17 − 3 − 3 = **11**

18 − 12 + 4 = **10**

ADDING AND SUBTRACTING

Reward
sticker!

Counting 1 – 10

Count how many things there are in each row.
Write your answers in the boxes.

Reward
sticker!

Reward sticker!

35

Counting 11 – 20

Count how many things there are in each row.
Write your answers in the boxes.

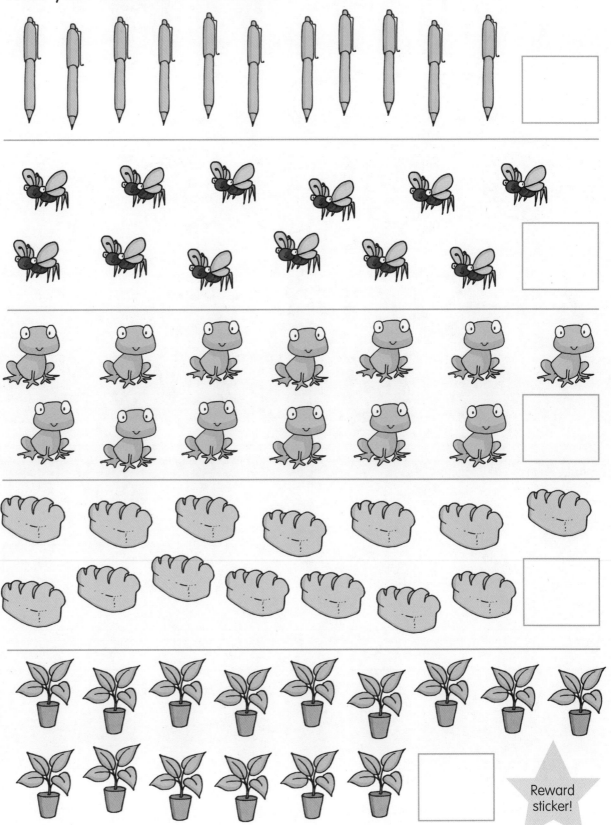

Reward
sticker!

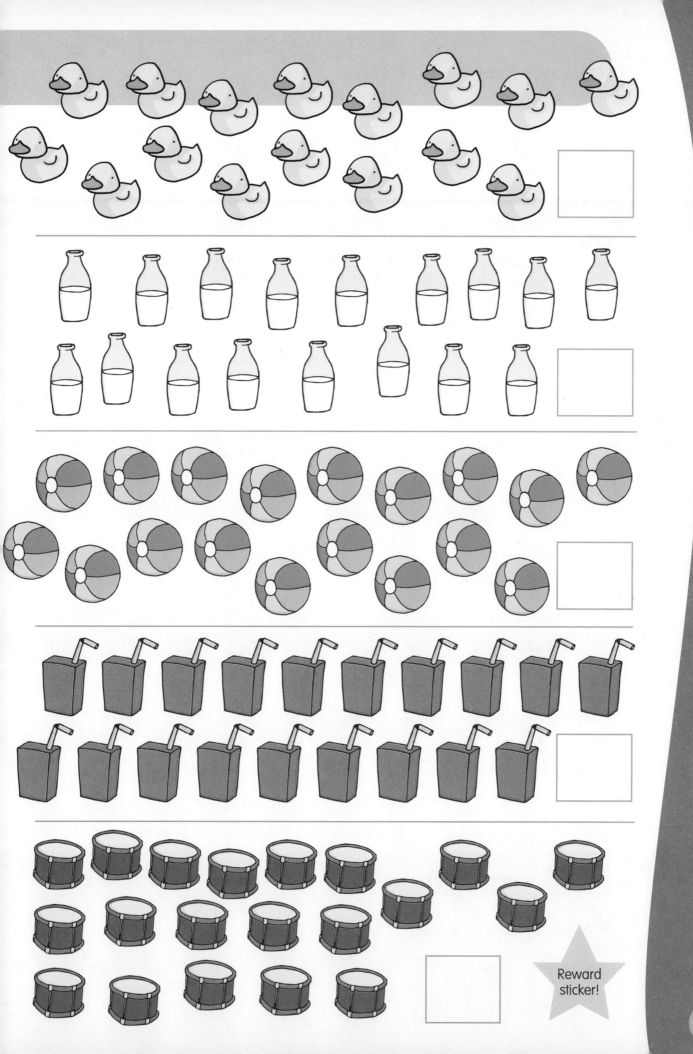

Reward sticker!

Adding one more

Using the pictures below, practice adding **one** more.
e.g. **3** apples + **1** apple = **4** apples.
Write your answers in the boxes.

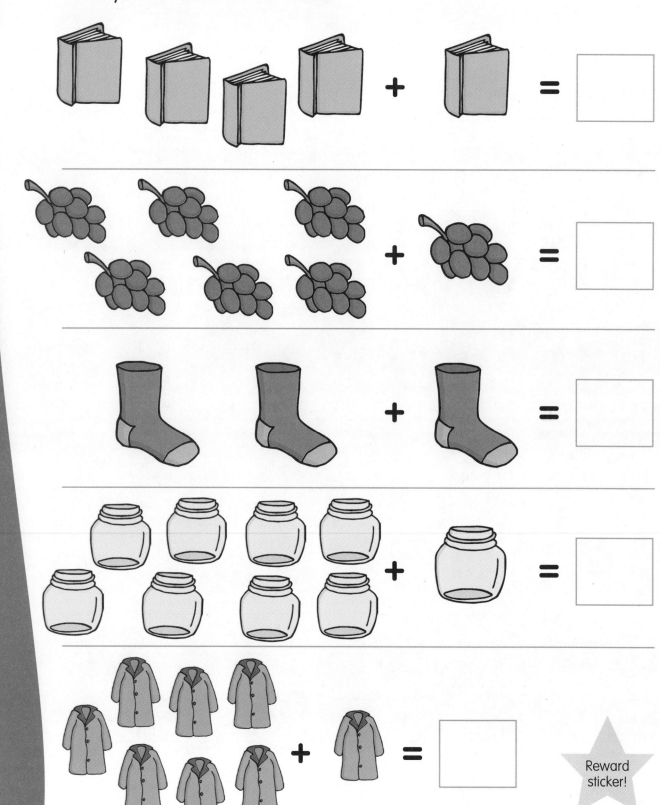

Reward
sticker!

Adding bigger numbers

Using the pictures below, practice adding **two**, **three** or **four** more.
e.g. **3** apples + **2** apples = **5** apples.
Write your answers in the boxes.

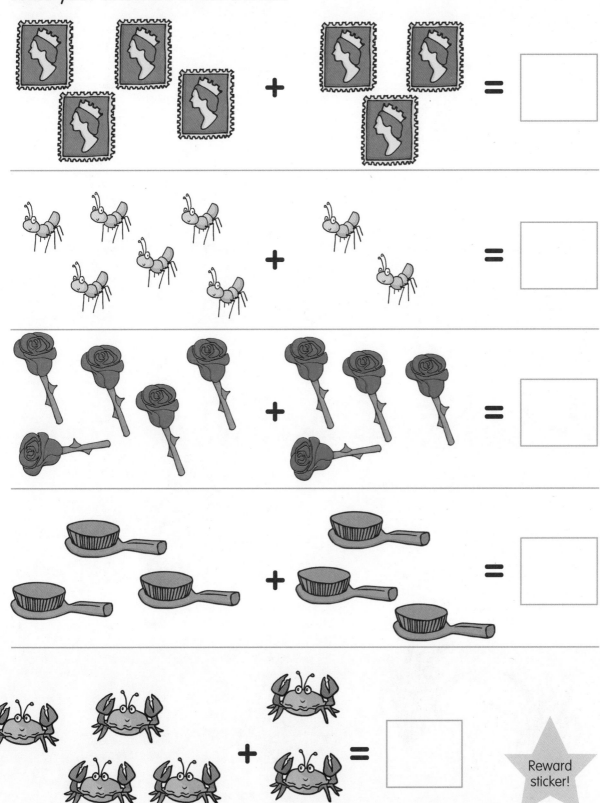

Reward
sticker!

Number bonds to 10

Solve these addition problems by adding the numbers together. Write your answers in the boxes.
What do you notice about the answers?

6 + 4 = ☐   3 + 7 = ☐

8 + 2 = ☐   9 + 1 = ☐

5 + 5 = ☐   7 + 3 = ☐

4 + 6 = ☐   2 + 8 = ☐

Reward
sticker!

Number bonds to 20

Solve these addition problems by adding the numbers together. Write your answers in the boxes.
What do you notice about the answers?

13 + 7 = ⬜   8 + 12 = ⬜

14 + 6 = ⬜   9 + 11 = ⬜

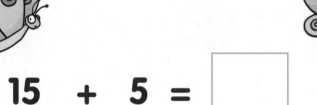

15 + 5 = ⬜   10 + 10 = ⬜

17 + 3 = ⬜   18 + 2 = ⬜

1 + 19 = ⬜   12 + 8 = ⬜

Reward sticker!

Super sums

Solve these addition problems by adding the numbers together.
Write your answers in the boxes.

4 + 3 = ☐   5 + 4 = ☐

2 + 6 = ☐   7 + 4 = ☐

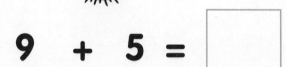

9 + 5 = ☐   7 + 8 = ☐

1 + 19 = ☐   2 + 8 = ☐

7 + 7 = ☐   6 + 9 = ☐

17 + 3 = ☐   10 + 3 = ☐

13 + 4 = ☐   2 + 9 = ☐

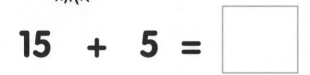

4 + 11 = ☐   3 + 5 = ☐

15 + 5 = ☐   7 + 12 = ☐

4 + 6 = ☐   13 + 6 = ☐

5 + 4 = ☐   12 + 5 = ☐

Reward
sticker!

Fact families

Here is a fact family for 2 + 8 = 10.

- 2 + 8 = 10
- 10 − 8 = 2
- 8 + 2 = 10
- 10 − 2 = 8

Complete the following fact families:

- 3 + 7 = 10
- ___ + ___ = ___
- ___ − ___ = ___
- ___ − ___ = ___

- 1 + 6 = 7
- ___ + ___ = ___
- ___ − ___ = ___
- ___ − ___ = ___

- 5 + 4 = 9
- ___ + ___ = ___
- ___ − ___ = ___
- ___ − ___ = ___

Reward sticker!

Here is a fact family for 4 + 3 = 7.

- **4 + 3 = 7**   - **3 + 4 = 7**
- **7 – 3 = 4**   - **7 – 4 = 3**

Complete the following fact families:

- **5 + 8 = 13**   - __ **+** __ **=** __

- __ **–** __ **=** __   - __ **–** __ **=** __

- **2 + 3 = 5**   - __ **+** __ **=** __

- __ **–** __ **=** __   - __ **–** __ **=** __

- **6 + 5 = 11**   - __ **+** __ **=** __

- __ **–** __ **=** __   - __ **–** __ **=** __

Reward sticker!

Missing numbers

Fill in the missing numbers to solve these addition problems.

e.g. 14 + **3** = 17

☐ + 4 = 7   ☐ + 2 = 8

5 + ☐ = 9   6 + ☐ = 11

☐ + 10 = 16   ☐ + 10 = 18

12 + ☐ = 15   14 + ☐ = 16

☐ + 13 = 18   ☐ + 11 = 19

Reward sticker!

Seeing double

Double the numbers below. Write your answers in the boxes.
Hint: 4 + 4 = 8 is the same as saying **double 4 = 8**.

Double **3** = ☐

Double **5** = ☐

Double **6** = ☐

Double **9** = ☐

Double **7** = ☐

Double **8** = ☐

Double **4** = ☐

Double **10** = ☐

Subtracting one

Using the pictures below, practice subtracting **one**.
e.g. **3** apples – **1** apple = **2** apples.
Write your answers in the boxes.

 =

 =

 =

 =

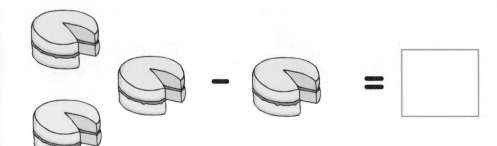 =

Reward
sticker!

Subtracting bigger numbers

Using the pictures below, practice subtracting **two**, **three** or **four**. e.g. **7** apples – **2** apples = **5** apples.
Write your answers in the boxes.

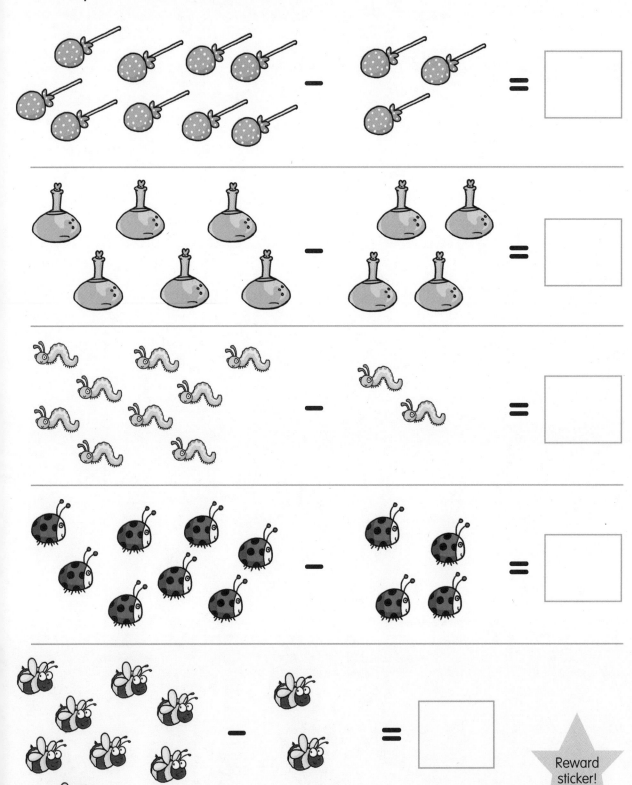

Reward sticker!

Subtracting from 10

Practice taking numbers away from 10 by doing the subtraction problems below. Write your answers in the boxes.

10 – 7 = ☐   10 – 4 = ☐

10 – 3 = ☐   10 – 8 = ☐

10 – 5 = ☐   10 – 2 = ☐

10 – 6 = ☐   10 – 1 = ☐

10 – 9 = ☐   10 – 10 = ☐

Reward sticker!

Super subtracting

Now practice taking **single** digit numbers from **two** digit numbers by completing these subtraction problems. Write your answers in the boxes.

17 − 6 =

18 − 5 =

19 − 4 =

17 − 3 =

16 − 5 =

14 − 6 =

12 − 5 =

13 − 7 =

15 − 8 =

18 − 9 =

Reward sticker!

Fact families

Here is a fact family for 9 – 6 = 3.

- 9 – 6 = 3
- 3 + 6 = 9
- 9 – 3 = 6
- 6 + 3 = 9

Complete the following fact families:

- 9 – 7 = 2
- ___ + ___ = ___
- ___ – ___ = ___
- ___ + ___ = ___

___

- 8 – 3 = 5
- ___ + ___ = ___
- ___ – ___ = ___
- ___ + ___ = ___

___

- 9 – 5 = 4
- ___ + ___ = ___
- ___ – ___ = ___
- ___ + ___ = ___

Reward sticker!

Here is a fact family for 7 – 1 = 6.

- 7 – 1 = 6   - 7 – 6 = 1
- 6 + 1 = 7   - 1 + 6 = 7

Complete the following fact families:

- 13 – 8 = 5   - ___ – ___ = ___

- ___ + ___ = ___   - ___ + ___ = ___

- 10 – 3 = 7   - ___ – ___ = ___

- ___ + ___ = ___   - ___ + ___ = ___

- 11 – 2 = 9   - ___ – ___ = ___

- ___ + ___ = ___   - ___ + ___ = ___

Reward sticker!

Subtracting superstar

Complete these problems and write your answers in the boxes.

6 – 4 = ☐ 9 – 3 = ☐

17 – 4 = ☐ 19 – 5 = ☐

14 – 8 = ☐ 9 – 8 = ☐

19 – 9 = ☐ 15 – 8 = ☐

10 – 7 = ☐ 15 – 9 = ☐

Reward sticker!

16 – 4 = [ ]   11 – 2 = [ ]

12 – 7 = [ ]   13 – 6 = [ ]

15 – 7 = [ ]   17 – 9 = [ ]

15 – 5 = [ ]   16 – 7 = [ ]

14 – 6 = [ ]   19 – 6 = [ ]

15 – 4 = [ ]   12 – 4 = [ ]

Reward sticker!

Subtracting from 20

Practice taking numbers away from **20** by doing the subtraction problems below. Write your answers in the boxes.

20 – 7 = ▢   20 – 4 = ▢

20 – 9 = ▢   20 – 6 = ▢

20 – 5 = ▢   20 – 14 = ▢

20 – 12 = ▢   20 – 17 = ▢

Reward sticker!

20 – 18 = ☐   20 – 13 = ☐

20 – 8 = ☐   20 – 16 = ☐

20 – 2 = ☐   20 – 19 = ☐

20 – 1 = ☐   20 – 11 = ☐

1 + 1 = 2
2 + 1 = 3
3 - 1 = 2
2 - 1 = 1

Reward sticker!

Amazing subtracting

Fill in the missing numbers to solve these subtraction problems.

e.g. **8 − 5 = 3**

8 − ☐ **= 2**   **6 −** ☐ **= 1**

☐ **− 8 = 11**   ☐ **− 3 = 14**

14 − ☐ **= 6**   **17 −** ☐ **= 8**

☐ **− 8 = 7**   ☐ **− 13 = 7**

Reward sticker!

12 - ☐ = 7   15 - ☐ = 6

☐ - 7 = 10   ☐ - 13 = 5

17 - ☐ = 2   14 - ☐ = 7

☐ - 9 = 10   ☐ - 10 = 8

16 - ☐ = 3   12 - ☐ = 6

Reward
sticker!

59

Halving

This activity is all about **halving** numbers. Try answering the questions below. **Hint:** half of **6 = 3** is the same as **6 − 3 = 3**.

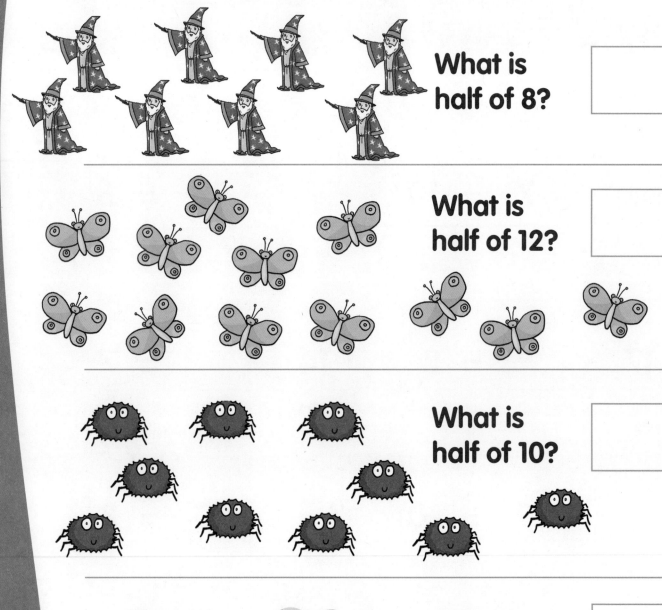

What is half of 8?

What is half of 12?

What is half of 10?

What is half of 16?

Reward sticker!

Test time!

Now you've worked through this section, test yourself on the following questions. Good luck!

+ =

+ =

3 + 7 = [ ]   8 + 12 = [ ]

Complete the following fact family:

- **4 + 6 = 10**   • ___ + ___ = ___

- ___ − ___ = ___   • ___ − ___ = ___

Double **9** = ☐   Double **6** = ☐

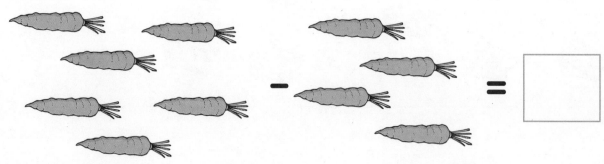 **–** = ☐

 – = ☐

10 – **7** = ☐   **17** – **6** = ☐

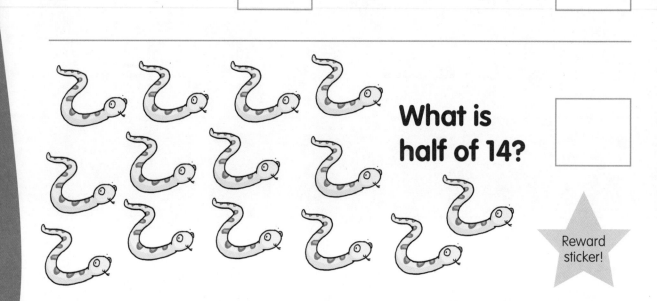 **What is half of 14?** ☐

Reward sticker!

Answers

Page 34–35: Counting 1 – 10
1, 2, 3, 4, 5, 6, 7, 8, 9, 10

Page 36–37: Counting 11 – 20
11, 12, 13, 14, 15, 16, 17, 18, 19, 20

Page 38: Adding one more
4 + 1 = **5**   8 + 1 = **9**

2 + 1 = **3**   7 + 1 = **8**

6 + 1 = **7**

Page 39: Adding bigger numbers
4 + 3 = **7**   3 + 3 = **6**

6 + 2 = **8**   4 + 2 = **6**

5 + 4 = **9**

Page 40: Number bonds to 10
6 + 4 = **10**   3 + 7 = **10**

8 + 2 = **10**   9 + 1 = **10**

5 + 5 = **10**   7 + 3 = **10**

4 + 6 = **10**   2 + 8 = **10**

Page 41: Number bonds to 20
13 + 7 = **20**   8 + 12 = **20**

14 + 6 = **20**   9 + 11 = **20**

15 + 5 = **20**   10 + 10 = **20**

17 + 3 = **20**   18 + 2 = **20**

1 + 19 = **20**   12 + 8 = **20**

Page 42–43: Super sums
4 + 3 = **7**   5 + 4 = **9**

2 + 6 = **8**   7 + 4 = **11**

9 + 5 = **14**   7 + 8 = **15**

1 + 19 = **20**   2 + 8 = **10**

7 + 7 = **14**   6 + 9 = **15**

17 + 3 = **20**   10 + 3 = **13**

13 + 4 = **17**   2 + 9 = **11**

4 + 11 = **15**   3 + 5 = **8**

15 + 5 = **20**   7 + 12 = **19**

4 + 6 = **10**   13 + 6 = **19**

5 + 4 = **9**   12 + 5 = **17**

Page 44–45: Fact families
3 + 7 = **10**   7 + **3** = **10**

10 - 7 = **3**   10 - **3** = **7**

1 + 6 = **7**   6 + **1** = **7**

7 - 6 = **1**   7 - **1** = **6**

5 + 4 = **9**   4 + **5** = **9**

9 - 4 = **5**   9 - **5** = **4**

5 + 8 = **13**   8 + **5** = **13**

13 - 8 = **5**   13 - **5** = **8**

2 + 3 = **5**   3 + **2** = **5**

5 - 3 = **2**   5 - **2** = **3**

6 + 5 = **11**   5 + **6** = **11**

11 - 5 = **6**   11 - **6** = **5**

Page 46: Missing numbers
3 + 4 = 7   **6** + 2 = 8

5 + **4** = 9   6 + **5** = 11

6 + 10 = 16   **8** + 10 = 18

12 + **3** = 15   14 + **2** = 16

5 + 13 = 18   8 + **11** = 19

Page 47: Seeing double
Double 3 = **6**   Double 5 = **10**

Double 6 = **12**   Double 9 = **18**

Double 7 = **14**   Double 8 = **16**

Double 4 = **8**   Double 10 = **20**

Page 48: Subtracting one
4 – 1 = **3**   8 – 1 = **7**

6 – 1 = **5**   3 – 1 = **2**

9 – 1 = **8**

Page 49: Subtracting bigger numbers
9 – 3 = **6**   8 – 4 = **4**

6 – 4 = **2**   8 – 2 = **6**

9 – 2 = **7**

Answers

Page 50: Subtracting from 10

$10 - 7 = 3$	$10 - 4 = 6$
$10 - 3 = 7$	$10 - 8 = 2$
$10 - 5 = 5$	$10 - 2 = 8$
$10 - 6 = 4$	$10 - 1 = 9$
$10 - 9 = 1$	$10 - 10 = 0$

Page 51: Super subtracting

$17 - 6 = 11$	$18 - 5 = 13$
$19 - 4 = 15$	$17 - 3 = 14$
$16 - 5 = 11$	$14 - 6 = 8$
$12 - 5 = 7$	$13 - 7 = 6$
$15 - 8 = 7$	$18 - 9 = 9$

Page 52: Fact families

$9 - 7 = 2$	$9 - 2 = 7$
$2 + 7 = 9$	$7 + 2 = 9$
$8 - 3 = 5$	$8 - 5 = 3$
$5 + 3 = 8$	$3 + 5 = 8$
$9 - 5 = 4$	$9 - 4 = 5$
$4 + 5 = 9$	$5 + 4 = 9$
$13 - 8 = 5$	$13 - 5 = 8$
$5 + 8 = 13$	$8 + 5 = 13$
$10 - 3 = 7$	$10 - 7 = 3$
$7 + 3 = 10$	$3 + 7 = 10$
$11 - 2 = 9$	$11 - 9 = 2$
$9 + 2 = 11$	$2 + 9 = 11$

Page 54: Subtracting superstar

$6 - 4 = 2$	$9 - 3 = 6$
$17 - 4 = 13$	$19 - 5 = 14$
$14 - 8 = 6$	$9 - 8 = 1$
$19 - 9 = 10$	$15 - 8 = 7$
$10 - 7 = 3$	$15 - 9 = 6$
$16 - 4 = 12$	$11 - 2 = 9$
$12 - 7 = 5$	$13 - 6 = 7$
$15 - 7 = 8$	$17 - 9 = 8$
$15 - 5 = 10$	$16 - 7 = 9$
$14 - 6 = 8$	$19 - 6 = 13$
$15 - 4 = 11$	$12 - 4 = 8$

Page 56: Subtracting from 20

$20 - 7 = 13$	$20 - 4 = 16$
$20 - 9 = 11$	$20 - 6 = 14$
$20 - 5 = 15$	$20 - 14 = 6$
$20 - 12 = 8$	$20 - 17 = 3$
$20 - 18 = 2$	$20 - 13 = 7$
$20 - 8 = 12$	$20 - 16 = 4$
$20 - 2 = 18$	$20 - 19 = 1$
$20 - 1 = 19$	$20 - 11 = 9$

Page 58: Amazing subtracting

$8 - 6 = 2$	$6 - 5 = 1$
$19 - 8 = 11$	$17 - 3 = 14$
$14 - 8 = 6$	$17 - 9 = 8$
$15 - 8 = 7$	$20 - 13 = 7$
$12 - 5 = 7$	$15 - 9 = 6$
$17 - 7 = 10$	$18 - 13 = 5$
$17 - 15 = 2$	$14 - 7 = 7$
$19 - 9 = 10$	$18 - 10 = 8$
$16 - 13 = 3$	$12 - 6 = 6$

Page 60: Halving

Half of $8 = 4$ Half of $12 = 6$
Half of $10 = 5$ Half of $16 = 8$

Page 61: Test time!

$4 + 1 = 5$	$5 + 4 = 9$
$3 + 7 = 10$	$8 + 12 = 20$
$4 + 6 = 10$	$6 + 4 = 10$
$10 - 6 = 4$	$10 - 4 = 6$

Page 62: Test time 2!

Double $9 = 18$ Double $6 = 12$

$8 - 1 = 7$	$6 - 4 = 2$
$10 - 7 = 3$	$17 - 6 = 11$

Half of $14 = 7$

MORE MATH

Reward sticker!

Counting forwards and backwards

Help the frogs get across the lily pads by filling in the missing numbers in these sequences:

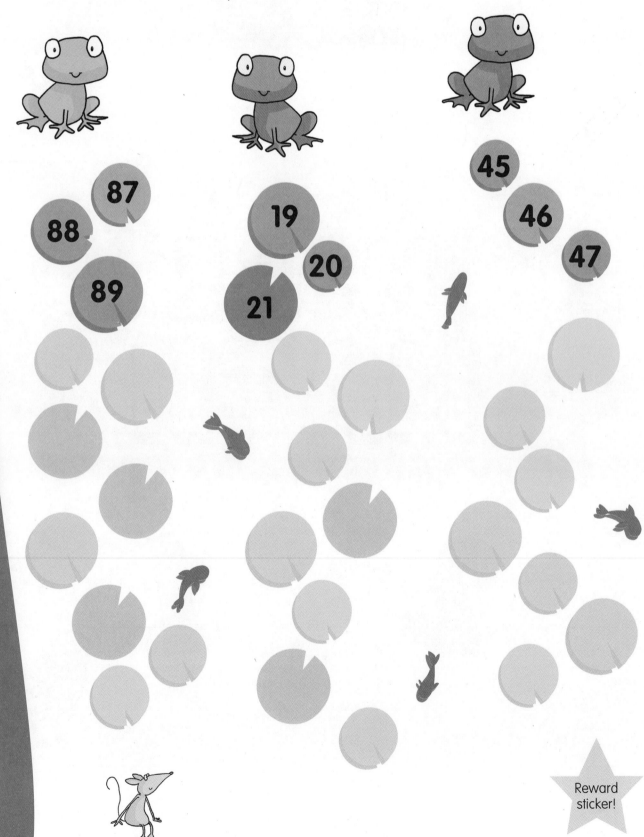

Reward sticker!

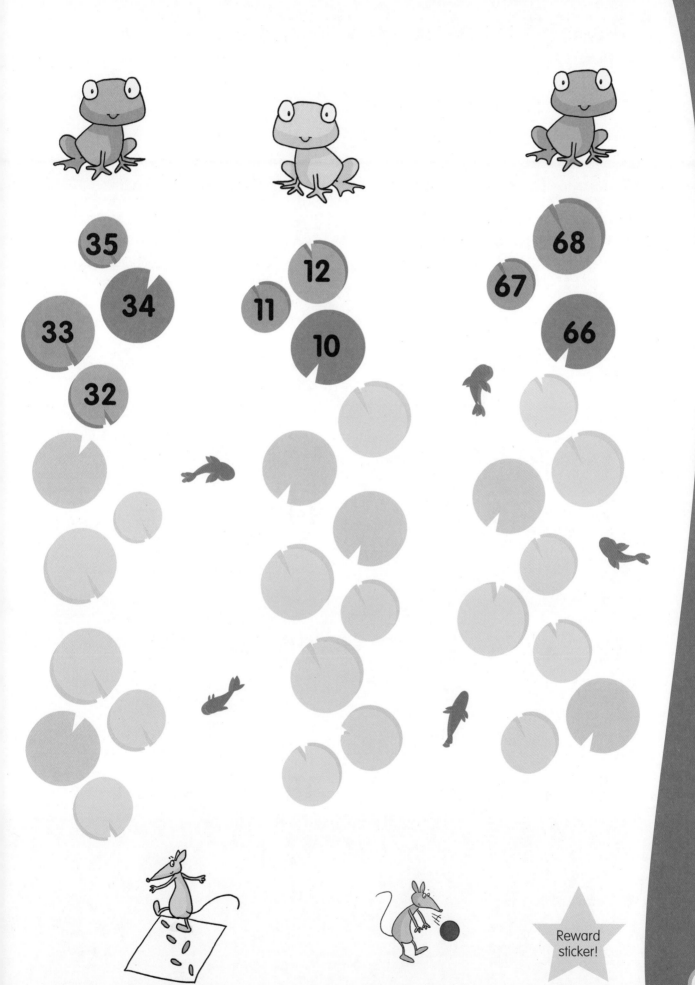

Reward sticker!

Addition and subtraction

Complete these addition and subtraction questions.
Write the answers in the boxes.

7 + 2 = [ ]   5 + 0 = [ ]

6 + 4 = [ ]   9 – 7 = [ ]

7 – 6 = [ ]   14 + 5 = [ ]

12 + 6 = [ ]   20 – 9 = [ ]

11 + 8 = [ ]   18 – 4 = [ ]

Reward
sticker!

7 + 11 = ☐   5 + 12 = ☐

4 + 18 = ☐   14 − 0 = ☐

17 − 5 = ☐   14 − 8 = ☐

16 − 8 = ☐   15 + 9 = ☐

19 − 10 = ☐   2 + 19 = ☐

Adding 10s

Complete the problems on the left, then use the fact in the blue box to work out the problems on the right.

> 4 + 3 = 7 so 40 + 30 = 70

5 + 2 = 7   so   50 + 20 = ☐

2 + 3 = ☐   so   20 + 30 = ☐

4 + 2 = ☐   so   40 + 20 = ☐

6 + 2 = ☐   so   60 + 20 = ☐

1 + 3 = ☐   so   10 + 30 = ☐

Reward sticker!

7 + 2 = ☐ so 70 + 20 = ☐

3 + 2 = ☐ so 30 + 20 = ☐

1 + 1 = ☐ so 10 + 10 = ☐

5 + 1 = ☐ so 50 + 10 = ☐

7 + 1 = ☐ so 70 + 10 = ☐

Missing numbers

Fill in the missing numbers to solve these addition and subtraction problems. There are two examples to start you off.

$6 + \boxed{4} = 10$ $9 - \boxed{3} = 6$

$\boxed{} + 4 = 9$ $\boxed{} - 6 = 5$

$12 + \boxed{} = 17$ $\boxed{} + 6 = 16$

$\boxed{} - 10 = 6$ $14 - \boxed{} = 6$

Reward sticker!

□ + 12 = 14   □ − 6 = 12

14 − □ = 1   □ + 8 = 20

19 − □ = 10   □ + 6 = 19

□ − 0 = 11   16 + □ = 18

Doubling

Double the numbers below. Write your answers in the boxes.
Hint: double 4 is the same as saying **4 x 2**, or **4 + 4**.

Double 1 = ⬜   Double 7 = ⬜

Double 9 = ⬜   Double 4 = ⬜

Double 2 = ⬜   Double 6 = ⬜

Double 8 = ⬜   Double 5 = ⬜

Double 3 = ⬜   Double 10 = ⬜

Reward sticker!

Now double these numbers. Write your answers in the boxes.
Hint: double 3 = 6, double 30 = 60.

Double 20 = ⬜ **Double 70 =** ⬜

Double 30 = ⬜ **Double 80 =** ⬜

Double 40 = ⬜ **Double 90 =** ⬜

Double 50 = ⬜ **Double 60 =** ⬜

Double 100 = ⬜

Reward sticker!

Order, order!

Put the numbers in the robot codes in order of **smallest** to **largest**.

3, 7, 2, 1, 5, 6, 4

16, 11, 15, 12, 14, 13, 10

55, 39, 63, 5, 56, 60, 15

Reward sticker!

Now put these numbers in order of **largest** to **smallest**.

67, 66, 61, 62, 65, 63, 64

82, 84, 85, 83, 87, 88, 86

93, 67, 88, 54, 11, 39, 9

All at odds

Circle all the **odd** numbers.

1
51
48
82
59
66
23
6
9
44
15
90
4
2
55
5
8
3
10

Reward sticker!

Get even!

Circle all the **even** numbers.

1
23
21
9
3
8
22
39
4
15
64
80
5
27
46
6
97
25
38
2
10

Shapes and fractions

Write the name of each **shape**, then color the **fraction**.

Color ½ of this shape.

C _ _ _ _ _ _

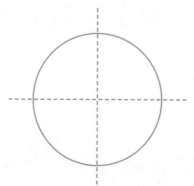

Color ¼ of this shape.

S _ _ _ _ _ _

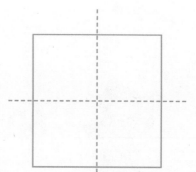

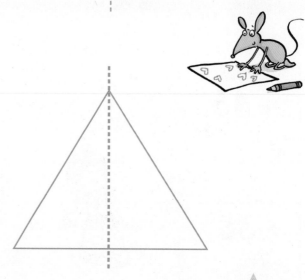

Color ½ of this shape.

T _ _ _ _ _ _ _ _

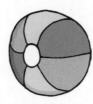

Reward sticker!

Color ¼ of this shape.

R _ _ _ _ _ _ _ _

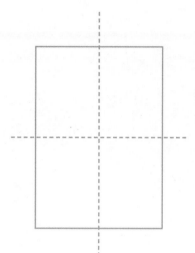

Color ¾ of this shape.

C _ _ _ _ _

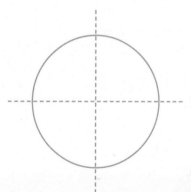

Counting in 2s and 10s

Continue these magical number sequences:

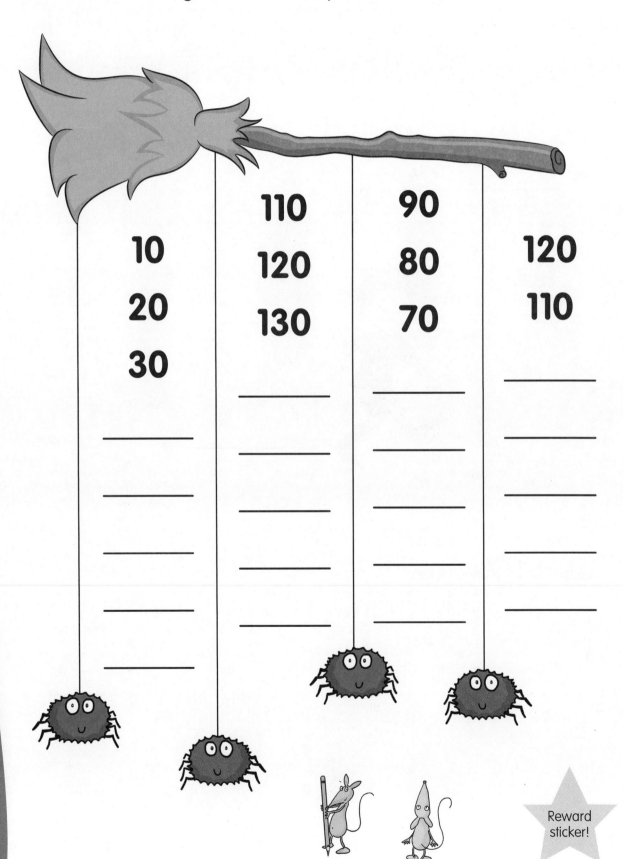

10	110	90	120
20	120	80	110
30	130	70	

Reward sticker!

0
2
4
___
___
___

10
8
6
___
___
___

24
22
___
___
___
___
___
___

16
14
___
___
___
___
___
___

Reward sticker!

83

10 times tables

Look at these multiplications and fill in the missing numbers.

1 x 10 = 10   10 x 10 = 100

2 x __ = 20   __ x 10 = 200

__ x 10 = 30   30 x 10 = ___

4 x 10 = __   40 x 10 = 400

__ x 10 = 50   50 x __ = 500

Reward
sticker!

Now try these:

11 x 10 =

14 x 10 =

16 x 10 =

21 x 10 =

19 x 10 =

43 x 10 =

Reward sticker!

Halve it!

Draw a ring around **half** of the group of objects for each question.
Next, answer the questions and write your answer in the box.

  **What is half of 2?**

 **What is half of 4?**

  **What is half of 6?**

    **What is half of 8?**

Reward sticker!

86

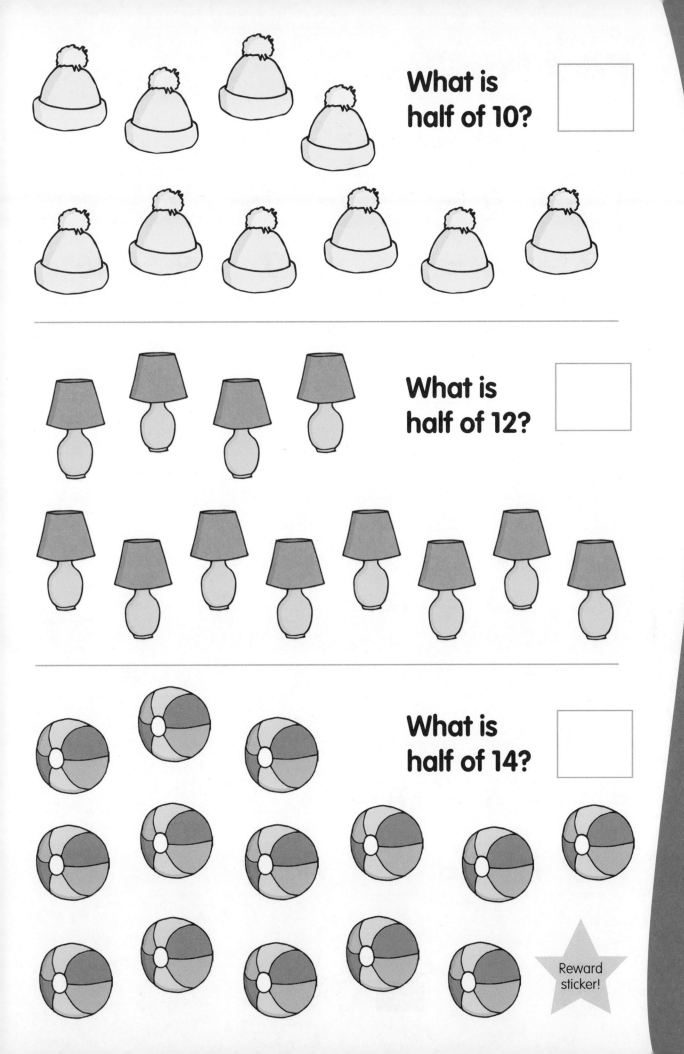

**What is
half of 10?**

**What is
half of 12?**

**What is
half of 14?**

Reward
sticker!

Fact families

Here is a fact family for **16 – 9 = 7**:

- 16 – 9 = 7
- 9 + 7 = 16
- 16 – 7 = 9
- 7 + 9 = 16

Complete the following fact families:

- **17 – 8 = 9**
- ___ + ___ = ___

- ___ – ___ = ___
- ___ + ___ = ___

- **15 – 3 = 12**
- ___ + ___ = ___

- ___ – ___ = ___
- ___ + ___ = ___

- **14 – 6 = 8**
- ___ + ___ = ___

- ___ – ___ = ___
- ___ + ___ = ___

Reward sticker!

Here is a fact family for **40 + 30 = 70**:

- **40 + 30 = 70**   • **30 + 40 = 70**
- **70 − 40 = 30**   • **70 − 30 = 40**

Complete the following fact families:

• **50 + 40 = 90**   • __ + __ = __

• __ − __ = __   • __ − __ = __

• **20 + 30 = 50**   • __ + __ = __

• __ − __ = __   • __ − __ = __

• **60 + 10 = 70**   • __ + __ = __

• __ − __ = __   • __ − __ = __

Reward sticker!

89

Missing numbers

Fill in the missing numbers to solve these **multiplication** questions.
Write your answers in the boxes. Some have been done for you.

3 x 2 = 6   so   30 x 20 = 600

4 x 2 =   so   40 x 20 =

8 x 2 =   so   80 x 20 =

10 x 2 =   so   100 x 20 =

9 x 2 =   so   90 x 20 =

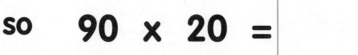

Reward sticker!

3 x 5 = 15   so   30 x 50 = 1500

5 x 5 =   so   50 x 50 =

2 x 5 =   so   20 x 50 =

7 x 5 =   so   70 x 50 =

9 x 5 =   so   90 x 50 =

1 x 5 =   so   10 x 50 =

6 x 5 =   so   60 x 50 =

Reward sticker!

Dividing by 2 and 5

Fill in the answers to these **division** questions.
Write your answers in the boxes.

$2 \div 2 = \boxed{}$ $12 \div 2 = \boxed{}$

$4 \div 2 = \boxed{}$ $14 \div 2 = \boxed{}$

$6 \div 2 = \boxed{}$ $16 \div 2 = \boxed{}$

$8 \div 2 = \boxed{}$ $18 \div 2 = \boxed{}$

$10 \div 2 = \boxed{}$ $20 \div 2 = \boxed{}$

Reward sticker!

5 ÷ 5 = ☐   30 ÷ 5 = ☐

10 ÷ 5 = ☐   35 ÷ 5 = ☐

15 ÷ 5 = ☐   40 ÷ 5 = ☐

20 ÷ 5 = ☐   45 ÷ 5 = ☐

25 ÷ 5 = ☐   50 ÷ 5 = ☐

Reward sticker!

93

Dividing by 10, 5, and 2

Fill in the answers to these **division** questions.
Write your answers in the boxes.

$20 \div 10 =$ [ ] $60 \div 10 =$ [ ]

$40 \div 10 =$ [ ] $90 \div 10 =$ [ ]

$50 \div 10 =$ [ ] $100 \div 10 =$ [ ]

$18 \div 2 =$ [ ] $60 \div 5 =$ [ ]

$110 \div 10 =$ [ ] $55 \div 5 =$ [ ]

Reward sticker!

Answers

Page 66–67: Counting forwards and backwards

87, 88, 89, **90, 91, 92, 93, 94, 95, 96, 97**

19, 20, 21, **22, 23, 24, 25, 26, 27, 28, 29**

45, 46, 47, **48, 49, 50, 51, 52, 53, 54**

35, 34, 33, 32, **31, 30, 29, 28, 27, 26, 25**

12, 11, 10, **9, 8, 7, 6, 5, 4, 3, 2**

68, 67, 66, **65, 64, 63, 62, 61, 60, 59, 58**

Page 68–69: Addition and subtraction

7 + 2 = **9**	5 + 0 = **5**
6 + 4 = **10**	9 – 7 = **2**
7 – 6 = **1**	14 + 5 = **19**
12 + 6 = **18**	20 – 9 = **11**
11 + 8 = **19**	18 – 4 = **14**
7 + 11 = **18**	5 + 12 = **17**
4 + 18 = **22**	14 – 0 = **14**
17 – 5 = **12**	14 – 8 = **6**
16 – 8 = **8**	15 + 9 = **24**
19 – 10 = **9**	2 + 19 = **21**

Page 70–71: Adding 10s

5 + 2 = **7**	50 + 20 = **70**
2 + 3 = **5**	20 + 30 = **50**
4 + 2 = **6**	40 + 20 = **60**
6 + 2 = **8**	60 + 20 = **80**
1 + 3 = **4**	10 + 30 = **40**
7 + 2 = **9**	70 + 20 = **90**
3 + 2 = **5**	30 + 20 = **50**
1 + 1 = **2**	10 + 10 = **20**
5 + 1 = **6**	50 + 10 = **60**
7 + 1 = **8**	70 + 10 = **80**

Page 72–73: Missing numbers

5 + 4 = 9	**11** – 6 = 5
12 + **5** = 17	**10** + 6 = 16
16 – 10 = 6	14 – **8** = 6
2 + 12 = 14	**18** – 6 = 12
14 – **13** = 1	**12** + 8 = 20
19 – **9** = 10	**13** + 6 = 19
11 – 0 = 11	16 + **2** = 18

Page 74–75: Doubling

Double 1 = **2**	Double 7 = **14**
Double 9 = **18**	Double 4 = **8**
Double 2 = **4**	Double 6 = **12**
Double 8 = **16**	Double 5 = **10**
Double 3 = **6**	Double 10 = **20**

Double 20 = **40**	Double 70 = **140**
Double 30 = **60**	Double 80 = **160**
Double 40 = **80**	Double 90 = **180**
Double 50 = **100**	Double 60 = **120**
Double 100 = **200**	

Page 76–77: Order, order!

1, 2, 3, 4, 5, 6, 7

10, 11, 12, 13, 14, 15, 16

5, 15, 39, 55, 56, 60, 63

67, 66, 65, 64, 63, 62, 61

88, 87, 86, 85, 84, 83, 82

93, 88, 67, 54, 39, 11, 9

Page 78: All at odds

1, 51, 59, 23, 9, 15, 55, 5, 3

Page 79: Get even!

8, 22, 4, 64, 6, 80, 46, 10, 2, 38

Page 80: Shapes and fractions

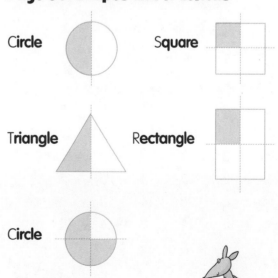

Circle

Square

Triangle

Rectangle

Circle

Answers

Page 82-83: Counting in 2s and 10s

10, 20, 30, **40, 50, 60, 70, 80**

110, 120, 130, **140, 150, 160, 170, 180**

90, 80, 70, **60, 50, 40, 30, 20**

120, 110, **100, 90, 80, 70, 60**

0, 2, 4, **6, 8, 10**

10, 8, 6, **4, 2, 0**

24, 22, **20, 18, 16, 14, 12, 10, 8, 6**

16, 14, **12, 10, 8, 6, 4, 2**

Page 84-85: 10 times tables

2 x **10** = 20	**20** x 10 = 200
3 x 10 = 30	30 x 10 = **300**
4 x 10 = **40**	40 x 10 = 400
5 x 10 = 50	50 x **10** = 500

11 x 10 = **110**

14 x 10 = **140**

16 x 10 = **160**

21 x 10 = **210**

19 x 10 = **190**

43 x 10 = **430**

Page 86: Halve it!

Half of 2 = **1**	Half of 10 = **5**
Half of 4 = **2**	Half of 12 = **6**
Half of 6 = **3**	Half of 14 = **7**
Half of 8 = **4**	

Page 88-89: Fact families

17 – 8 = 9	**17 – 9 = 8**
8 + 9 = 17	9 + 8 = 17
15 – 3 = 12	**15 – 12 = 3**
3 + 12 = 15	12 + 3 = 15
14 – 6 = 8	**14 – 8 = 6**
6 + 8 = 14	8 + 6 = 14

50 + 40 = 90	**40 + 50 = 90**
90 – 50 = 40	**90 – 40 = 50**
20 + 30 = 50	**30 + 20 = 50**
50 – 30 = 20	**50 – 20 = 30**
60 + 10 = 70	**10 + 60 = 70**
70 – 60 = 10	**70 – 10 = 60**

Page 90-91: Missing numbers

3 x 2 = 6	30 x 20 = 600
4 x 2 = **8**	40 x 20 = **800**
8 x 2 = **16**	80 x 20 = **1600**
10 x 2 = **20**	100 x 20 = **2000**
9 x 2 = **18**	90 x 20 = **1800**

3 x 5 = 15	30 x 50 = 1500
5 x 5 = **25**	50 x 50 = **2500**
2 x 5 = **10**	20 x 50 = **1000**
7 x 5 = **35**	70 x 50 = **3500**
9 x 5 = **45**	90 x 50 = **4500**
1 x 5 = **5**	10 x 50 = **500**
6 x 5 = **30**	60 x 50 = **3000**

Page 92-93: Dividing by 2 and 5

2 ÷ 2 = **1**	12 ÷ 2 = **6**
4 ÷ 2 = **2**	14 ÷ 2 = **7**
6 ÷ 2 = **3**	16 ÷ 2 = **8**
8 ÷ 2 = **4**	18 ÷ 2 = **9**
10 ÷ 2 = **5**	20 ÷ 2 = **10**

5 ÷ 5 = **1**	30 ÷ 5 = **6**
10 ÷ 5 = **2**	35 ÷ 5 = **7**
15 ÷ 5 = **3**	40 ÷ 5 = **8**
20 ÷ 5 = **4**	45 ÷ 5 = **9**
25 ÷ 5 = **5**	50 ÷ 5 = **10**

Page 94: Dividing by 10, 5, and 2

20 ÷ 10 = **2**	60 ÷ 10 = **6**
40 ÷ 10 = **4**	90 ÷ 10 = **9**
50 ÷ 10 = **5**	100 ÷ 10 = **10**
18 ÷ 2 = **9**	60 ÷ 5 = **12**
110 ÷ 10 = **11**	55 ÷ 5 = **11**

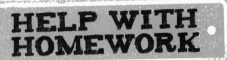

READING & WRITING

Reward
sticker!

Alphabet blocks

Finish writing the letters of the alphabet on these blocks.
Then look at the objects. What letters do they begin with?
Draw lines to join each object to the correct letter.

Reward
sticker!

Finish the rhyme

Complete the nursery rhyme below by working out which of the words in the boxes goes in each blank.

ten   finger   four   go   you

One, two, three, _____ , five.

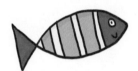

Once I caught a fish alive.

Six, seven, eight, nine, _____ .

Then I let it _____ again.

Why did _____ let it go?

Because it bit my finger so.

Which _____ did it bite?

This little finger on the right.

Find the vowels

Vowels are the letters **a**, **e**, **i**, **o** and **u**. Find them below and circle them. There are **25** in total.

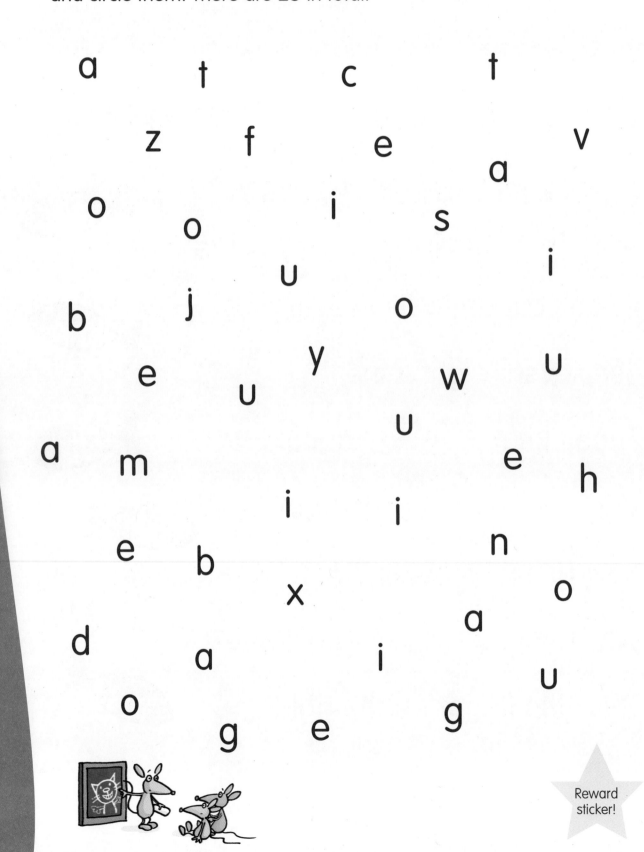

Reward sticker!

Find the consonants

Consonants are letters that are not vowels. Find them below and circle them. There are **25** in total.

Reward sticker!

Missing vowels

Fill in the missing vowels to complete the words below.
Hint: The vowels are **a**, **e**, **i**, **o** and **u**.

c__t

b__d

f__n

d__g

m__g

h__n

n__t

b__x

k__ng

fl__g

fr__g

dr__m

sh__p

h__rp

m__st

sw__m

Missing consonants

Write the correct consonant at the start of each word.
Hint: Consonants are letters that are not vowels.

__rog

__ree

__ocket

__able

__ar

__lock

__ock

__rab

__rush

Labels

Labels can be used on pictures to help us understand the information. Write the correct labels in the empty boxes below, using these words.

neck   leg   horn   ear

hoof   tail

Reading and writing

Look at the pictures below. Under each one is a sentence with a word missing. Choose the correct word from the boxes below and write it in.

| books | cat | balloons | tree |

The _____ is chasing the dog.

Erin likes sitting in the _____.

Joe and Samir have

_____.

Jason loves

_____.

Reading and matching

Write the correct sentence beside each picture.

- The boys are carefully holding their balloons.
- The scared dog is being chased by a cat!
- Erin is hiding in the tall tree.
- Jason is quietly reading his book.

1. _____

_____

2. _____

_____

3. _____

_____

4. _____

_____

Reward sticker!

Capital letters

Words that are the names of people or places are given **capital letters**. These words are called **proper nouns**. Look at the words below and circle the ones that should have capital letters.

computer

olivia

england

hippo

illinois

james

france

canada

apple

trees

bicycle

boat

book

carrot

fiona

Now look at the sentences below and circle the words that should have **capital letters**. Remember the first word of any sentence should also start with a capital letter.

a flag flutters in sean's hand.

julia would like to go to america.

surriya is going to pakistan to see her grandparents.

falling leaves and acorns remind chris of fall.

the birds fly all the way to africa in winter.

Now write your own sentence using capital letters. Try to make sure it includes the name of a person and a place.

_____

_____

_____

Periods

We finish sentences with a **period**. Arrange the words below into sentences, and add a period at the end of each one.

James football played

_____

Australia Kangaroos in live

_____

wet and cold is December

_____

Susan two brothers Jim and Niall named has

_____

It's your turn to be the teacher! Get a red pencil and put a circle around the letters that should have **capital letters** and write in the **periods**.

1. "i like porridge," goldilocks muttered as she ran away

2. hippos and giraffes live in africa

3. if I lived at the north pole i might see santa claus

4. the capital city of england is london

5. pete has 3 brothers: joseph, patrick, and andy. they live in chicago

6. the space rocket flew to jupiter

Reward sticker!

Question marks

We use **question marks** to show that we are asking something. Do you see that dot under the squiggle? A question mark goes at the end of a sentence instead of a period. Trace over the following question marks and finish the row.

Read the following sentences. Some are asking you something. You need to put a question mark after these ones. The others are statements. They tell you something and just need a period.

1. What is your favorite color

2. I don't like ice cream

3. Birds fly through the air

4. Do you want to go to the park

5. Which cake would you like

6. Africa and Asia are both continents

Reward sticker!

Commas

We use **commas** for different reasons. One of the reasons is when we list things. Commas go in between the things in the list, e.g. 'I went to the shop and I bought an apple, a banana, a pear, and an orange.' Don't forget to add **'and'** before the last item in the list.

Fill in the gaps with nouns (words for things). Choose whatever you like!

I went to the shop and I bought a

_____, a _____,

and a _____.

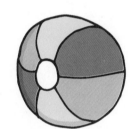

I went on holiday and I took a

_____, a _____,

and a _____.

For my birthday I would like a

_____, a _____,

and a _____.

Reward sticker!

Punctuation

Read the passage. Write in the missing **commas** and circle any words that should have **capital letters**. Can you spot any questions that should be followed by a **question mark**? If so, put them in!

Susan put her hand in her bag

She was surprised to find a

book an apple and a big monkey.

How could they have got there

what else would she find

could the bag be magic

What would you expect to find in your school bag? Write a sentence below using capital letters and commas.

_____

_____

_____

Reward sticker!

Write a postcard

Imagine you are on vacation at the beach. Write a message to your friend to say what you are doing.

Today I went to the beach.

_____

_____

_____

_____

Reward sticker!

Comprehension

Read the Little Red Riding Hood story below and answer the questions on the opposite page.

1.

Little Red Riding Hood decided to visit her sick grandmother.

2.

When she was picking some flowers in the forest, she met a wolf.

3.

When Little Red Riding Hood arrived at the house, the wolf had dressed up as her grandmother.

4.

"My, what big teeth you have," said Little Red Riding Hood.
"All the better to eat you with!" cried the wolf.

5.

6.

The wolf leaped out of bed and jumped on poor Little Red Riding Hood.

Luckily, a woodcutter was passing by and rescued her from the wicked wolf.

1. Who was Little Red Riding Hood going to visit?

_____

2. Who did she meet in the forest?

_____

3. What was she doing when she met the wolf?

_____

4. Who did the wolf pretend to be?

_____

5. Who saved Little Red Riding Hood?

_____

Reward sticker!

Writing stories

Read the passage of text below. Write the next two sentences to continue the story. What do you think happens next?

Eli walked down the path, through the shaded trees. He could hear the birds singing. Eli wondered what the birds were saying. Then, he heard a voice saying, "Hello Eli!" Eli couldn't see anyone, so he walked on. Suddenly he heard a crunch on the path. He turned and there stood a bear. A small bear, wearing a hat and a pair of sunglasses. It waved, smiled, and stepped slowly toward him.

_____

_____

_____

_____

Describe it

Some words help us to **describe** things, such as the **small** dog or the **sweet** apple. These words are called **adjectives**. Find the describing words below and circle them.

The small boy ate the big apple.

A fluffy cat sat in the red basket.

The dark clouds made the afternoon gloomy and dull.

The scary lion gave a loud roar and shook his

orange mane.

Now write your own sentence using as many adjectives as you can.

_____

_____

_____

Reward sticker!

Descriptive writing

Describe the picture below in two sentences. Make sure that you use **adjectives** to make your writing more interesting.

_____

_____

_____

_____

_____

Reward
sticker!

Alphabetical order

Look at the words below. Put them in alphabetical order.
Then draw lines to join each word to the correct image.

a b c d e f g h i j k l m n o p q r s t u v w x y z

tent   mitten   witch   tree

lamp   clown   duck

Reward
sticker!

Reading non-fiction

Read the passage below and answer the questions.

Giraffes are the tallest land animals. A giraffe could look into a second-floor window without even having to stand on its tiptoes! A giraffe's neck is 6 feet long. The legs of a giraffe are also 6 feet long. The back legs look shorter than the front legs, but they are actually about the same length.

Giraffes live in Africa. Some giraffes from Kenya have spots that are shaped like oak leaves. Some scientists think that the giraffe's pattern is for camouflage.

Both male and female giraffes have two hair-covered horns. Male giraffes use their horns to fight with one another. They are quite shy animals. Giraffes have blue-colored tongues. This is because they eat a lot of leaves. They use their tongues to rip the leaves off the trees, so their tongues spend a long time in the sun. Because they are a blue color, they don't get sunburnt!

Reward sticker!

1. What are the tallest land animals?

_____

2. How long is a giraffe's neck?

_____

3. Where do giraffes live?

_____

4. What type of leaves do the spots sometimes look like?

_____

5. How many horns does a giraffe have?

_____

6. What color is a giraffe's tongue?

_____

7. How does this help giraffes?

_____

Reward
sticker!

Read this poster about a circus that is coming to town.

★ ★ ★ ★ ★

The Big Top Circus
presents

Fred the fearless fire-eater,
Justin the juggler,
Clive the clown,
Tracey the trapeze artist,
Alan the acrobat,
and lots, lots more.

Join us at the Big Top for a
fun-filled evening to remember!

Date: Saturday July 3rd
Time: 7pm Place: Woodside Park
Price: Adults $2.50   Children $1.75

Reward
sticker!

Using the information from the poster, answer the questions below by putting a check in the correct box.

1. What is the name of the circus?

☐ Small Top ☐ Big Top

☐ Big Hat

2. What is Alan's job?

☐ An acrobat ☐ A clown

☐ A juggler

3. Who is the trapeze artist?

☐ Tracey ☐ Tara

☐ Alan

4. What time does the show start?

☐ 6pm ☐ 7am

☐ 7pm

5. How much are tickets for children?

☐ $1.75 ☐ $2.20

☐ $17.50

Reward sticker!

More questions

Read the poster on page 124 again.
Now answer these questions.

1. Where is the circus being held?

_____

2. Why is Fred described as fearless?

_____

3. What else do you think you might see at the circus?

_____

4. Would you rather be a clown, a juggler,
a fire-eater or a trapeze artist?

_____

5. Why?

_____

_____

_____

Writing practice

Can you make these sentences more interesting by adding detail and description?

E.g. The worm was in the earth ➜
The long, thin wriggly worm squirmed into the warm earth.

The leaves fell from the tree.

_____

_____

James bought a cake.

_____

_____

Answers:

Page 98: Alphabet blocks
ball, **c**hair, **d**rum, **f**ork, **t**ree, **s**tamp,

Page 99: Finish the rhyme
four, ten, go, you, finger

Pages 102–103: Missing vowels
c**a**t, b**e**d, f**a**n, d**o**g, m**u**g, h**e**n, n**u**t, b**o**x, k**i**ng, fl**a**g, fr**o**g, dr**u**m, sh**i**p, h**a**rp, m**a**st, sw**i**m

Page 104: Missing consonants
frog, **t**ree, **r**ocket, **t**able, **c**ar, **c**lock, **s**ock, **c**rab, **b**rush

Page 105: Labels

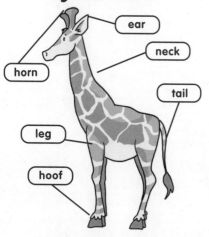

ear
neck
horn
tail
leg
hoof

Page 106: Reading and writing
cat, tree, balloons, books

Page 107: Reading and matching
1. The scared dog is being chased by a cat!
2. Jason is quietly reading his book.
3. The boys are carefully holding their balloons.
4. Erin is hiding in the tall tree.

Page 108–109: Capital letters
Olivia, England, Illinois, James, France, Canada, Fiona
A flag flutters in Sean's hand.
Julia would like to go to America.
Surriya is going to Pakistan to see her grandparents.
Falling leaves and acorns remind Chris of fall.
The birds fly all the way to Africa in winter.

Page 110–111: Periods
James played football.
Kangaroos live in Australia.
December is cold and wet.
Susan has two brothers named Jim and Niall.

1. "I like porridge," Goldilocks muttered as she ran away.
2. Hippos and giraffes live in Africa.
3. If I lived at the North Pole I might see Santa Claus.
4. The capital city of England is London.
5. Pete has 3 brothers: Joseph, Patrick, and Andy. They live in Chicago.
6. The space rocket flew to Jupiter.

Page 112: Question marks
1. What is your favorite color?
2. I don't like ice cream.
3. Birds fly through the air.
4. Do you want to go to the park?
5. Which cake would you like?
6. Africa and Asia are both continents.

Page 114: Punctuation
Susan put her hand in her bag. She was surprised to find a book, an apple, and a big monkey. How could they have got there? What else would she find? Could the bag be magic?

Page 116–117: Comprehension
1. She was visiting her sick grandmother.
2. She met a wolf.
3. She was picking some flowers.
4. The wolf pretended to be her grandmother.
5. A woodcutter saved her.

Page 119: Describe it
The small boy ate the big apple.
A fluffy cat sat in the red basket.
The dark clouds made the afternoon gloomy and dull.
The scary lion gave a loud roar and shook his orange mane.

Page 121: Alphabetical order
clown, duck, lamp, mitten, tent, tree, witch

Page 122–123: Reading non-fiction
1. Giraffes are the tallest land animal.
2. A giraffe's neck is 6 feet.
3. Giraffes live in Africa.
4. The spots are sometimes shaped like oak leaves.
5. Giraffes have two horns.
6. Giraffes have blue tongues.
7. They don't get sunburnt.

Page 124–125: Roll up! Roll up!
1. Big Top.
2. An acrobat.
3. Tracey.
4. 7pm.
5. $1.75.

Page 126: More questions
1. The circus is being held at Woodside Park.
2. He eats fire.
3. Example answers: tightrope walker, ringmaster, strongman

PHONICS

Reward
sticker!

First letter sounds

Look at the pictures. The first letters are missing.
Say the word, sound it out, and write in the missing letter.

__nt

__an

__og

__ish

__et

__at

__oot

__gg

__at

__ent

__enguin

__un

More first letter sounds

Look at the pictures. The first letters are missing. Say the word, sound it out, and write in the missing letter.

__anana

__up

__an

__one

__ctopus

Reward sticker!

End letter sounds

Look at the pictures. The last letters are missing. Say the word, sound it out, and write in the missing letter.

fro__

ja__

mo__

ca__

hamste__

bir__

More end letter sounds

Look at the pictures. The last letters are missing. Say the word, sound it out, and write in the missing letter.

fla___

we___

fo___

su___

he___

cra___

First and last sounds

Look at the pictures. The first and last letters are missing. Say the word, sound it out, and write in the missing letters.

__oo__

__low__

__oo__

__emo__

__am__

__o__

135

Find the missing sounds

Look at the pictures. The first sounds are missing. These sounds are made up of two letters. Say the word, sound it out, and write in the missing letters. You can choose from **sh**, **qu** or **ch**.

sh   qu   ch

___ick

___ip

___een

___eese

___air

___ark

More end letter sounds

Look at the pictures. The last sounds are missing. These sounds are made up of two letters. Say the word, sound it out, and write in the missing letters. You can choose from **nk**, **ng** or **ck**.

nk

ng

ck

ki___

dri___

ri___

cli___

thi___

Rhyming words

Rhyming words sound the same at the ends of the words, like box and fox. Look at the pictures and the words underneath. Match the rhyming words together by drawing a line between them.

bat

clock

van

hat

king

pan

sock

wing

Reward sticker!

mug

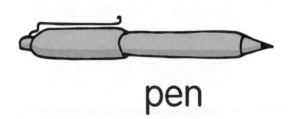

pen

10

ten

boy

frog

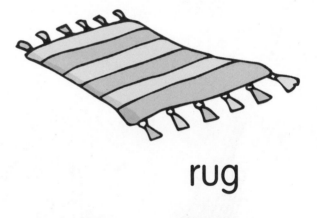

rug

toy

dog

Reward sticker!

Middle letter sounds

Look at the pictures. Say the word, sound it out, and work out what the missing sound is. Write the letter in the space.

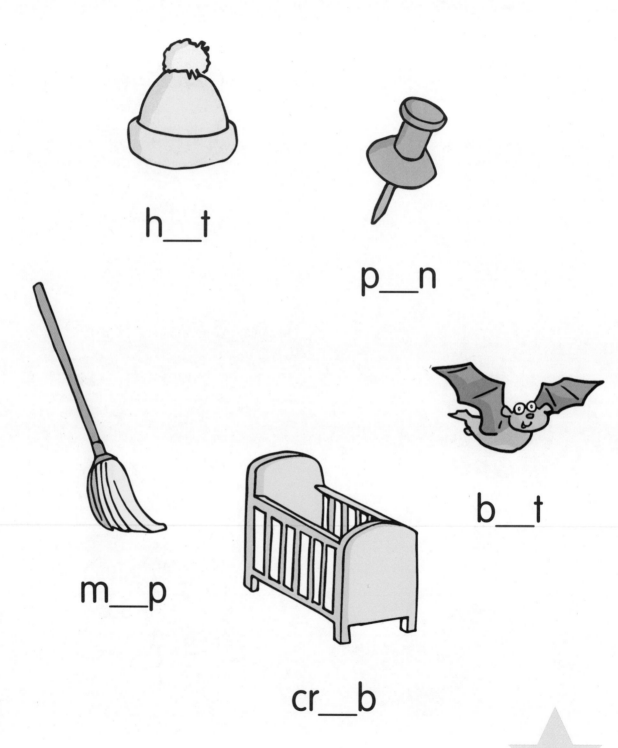

h__t

p__n

m__p

cr__b

b__t

Consonant blends

When two letters are put together to make one sound, they make a digraph. The digraphs below are made by blending two consonants. Choose from the tiles below to fill in the blanks.

fr

br

cr

cl

pl

fl

gl

__ead

__og

__y

__ant

__oud

__ue

__ab

Reward sticker!

More blending

Fill in the blanks with the correct consonant blends.
Choose from the tiles below.

st   sn   cr   cl   gr   dr   fl

___ick

___ink

___airs

___own

___owman

___ower

___apes

Reward sticker!

Ending blending

Fill in the blank at the end of each word with the correct consonant blend. Choose from the tiles below.

ck

nd

mp

lk

sh

nt

fi___

du___

te___

ha___

clo___

sta___

mi___

la___

a___

Reward sticker!

Is it 'ou' or 'oo'?

Write the names of the objects below underneath each picture.
Which words make an **ou** sound and which make an **oo** sound?

h_____

b_____

m_____

m_____

Is it 'ou' or 'ow'?

Each of the objects below makes use of either an **ou** or an **ow** sound. Write each object's name in the correct box, depending on which sound it uses.

OU

OW

Reward sticker!

Is it 'oy' or 'oi'?

Each of the objects below makes use of either an **oy** or an **oi** sound. Write each object's name in the correct box, depending on which sound it uses.

1 cent

oi

oy

Reward sticker!

Is it 'ow' or 'oa'?

Look at the pictures. All of the words either make use of an **ow** or an **oa** sound. Write each object's name in the correct place, using the words in the boxes to help you.

a.

b.

c.

d.

e.

arrow

goat

window

snow

coat

Is it 'ay' or 'ai'?

Look at the words below. You can choose either **ay** or **ai** to go in the missing spaces. Complete the words by filling in the blanks using the correct spelling.

st___

r__n

w___

tr__n

p__nt

d___

pl___

w__t

tr___

Reward sticker!

The 'igh' combination

Together, the letters **igh** make a sound like a long i. Complete the words below by adding **igh** to fill in the gaps.

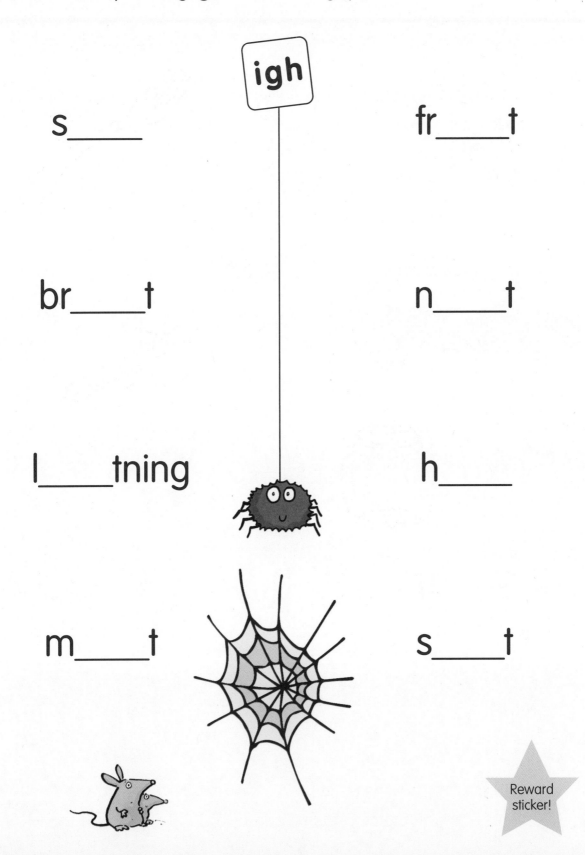

s____

fr____t

br____t

n____t

l____tning

h____

m____t

s____t

Reward sticker!

149

Is it 'ar' or 'or'?

Each of the objects below makes use of either an **ar** or an **or** sound. Write each object's name in the correct box, depending on which sound it uses.

or

ar

Reward sticker!

Is it 'air' or 'ir'?

Write the correct sounds into the words below. You can choose either **air** or **ir** to go in the missing spaces.

air

ir

st___

b___d

f___

ecl___

ch___

g___l

Get sketching

Read the words out loud, choose one from each group and draw a picture of it in the frame.

Group 1:

cake
face
snake
lake

Group 2:

mice bike
rice slice

Group 3:

mole
hole
stone
phone

Reward sticker!

Wordsearch

Can you find the words with **ee**, **oo** and **ar** sounds in the grid below?

d	e	v	z	l	m	a	r	k	p
a	s	d	f	s	p	o	o	n	g
h	p	a	r	t	j	k	b	x	l
z	x	c	v	a	b	n	m	q	a
w	s	c	t	r	e	e	d	c	r
f	v	t	g	b	y	h	n	u	b
j	m	i	h	k	m	e	e	t	e
o	l	z	o	p	o	q	l	w	a
a	s	j	o	w	o	g	j	d	k
s	e	a	t	b	n	f	h	q	a

tree   moon   star

seat   spoon   mark

beak   hoot

meet   part

Which spelling?

Finish each sentence by writing the word with the correct spelling in the blank. Remember to add a period!

A small animal with a long tail is called a _____

mouse	moose
mowse	mous

A man who wears a crown and lives in a palace is called a

_____

cing	knig
king	ching

When you don't wash your hands, they get _____

durty	derty
birty	dirty

Reward sticker!

An animal with a long trunk is called an _____

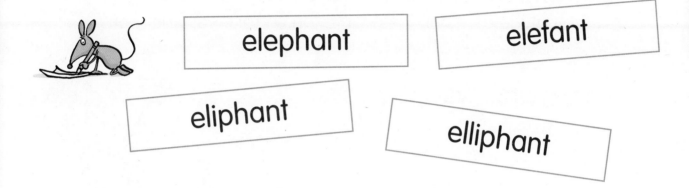

| elephant | elefant |
| eliphant | elliphant |

When you are walking in the woods, you must follow the

_____

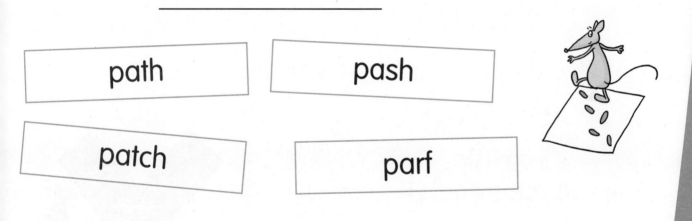

| path | pash |
| patch | parf |

Someone who lives on a farm is a _____

| pharmer | farmer |
| former | fermer |

You're the teacher!

Look at the sentences below. Which are correct?
Give them a checkmark if they are correct, or circle any
mistakes if they are not. Then write the correct word beneath.

a. The nurse was very noysy.

b. Our garden has a lot of trees.
There are also a lot of birds.

c. Once upon a time there was a prinsess.

d. Five yeers ago, we moved to
Maryland.

e. Wen will it be time to go home?

Reward
sticker!

Nonsense words

Using the consonant pairs below and some vowels, make up some nonsense words that could describe a fruit. You might describe how they look, taste, smell, or feel.

E.g. That apple smells **flurpy** or that pear tastes **glucky**!

fl ch ck rp st gr le y o e a u i

_____

_____

Reward
sticker!

More nonsense words

Circle the words below that are nonsense words. Then, pick your favorite nonsense word and draw a picture of how you imagine it might look in the frame opposite.

robot

kear

vurk   queen

boot   kite

chick

queck

jigh

thorden

zurd

coat

duck

nud

kitten   flurp

plab

Reward sticker!

Reward sticker!

Answers:

Page 130: First letter sounds

<u>a</u>nt, <u>p</u>an, <u>d</u>og, <u>f</u>ish, <u>n</u>et, <u>r</u>at, <u>b</u>oot, <u>h</u>at, <u>e</u>gg, <u>t</u>ent, <u>s</u>un, <u>p</u>enguin

Page 132: More first letter sounds

<u>b</u>anana, <u>f</u>an, <u>c</u>up, <u>b</u>one, <u>o</u>ctopus

Page 133: End letter sounds

ja<u>r</u>, fro<u>g</u>, mo<u>p</u>, hamste<u>r</u>, ca<u>t</u>, bir<u>d</u>

Page 134: More end letter sounds

fla<u>g</u>, we<u>b</u>, fo<u>x</u>, su<u>n</u>, he<u>n</u>, cra<u>b</u>

Page 135: First and last sounds

<u>moon</u>, <u>c</u>lown, <u>book</u>, <u>l</u>emo<u>n</u>, <u>box</u>, lamp

Page 136: Find the missing sounds

<u>ch</u>ick, <u>sh</u>ip, <u>qu</u>een, <u>ch</u>eese, <u>ch</u>air, <u>sh</u>ark

Page 137: More end letter sounds

ki<u>ng</u>, dri<u>nk</u>, ri<u>ng</u>, cli<u>ck</u>, thi<u>nk</u>

Page 138–139: Rhyming words

bat + hat, clock + sock, van + pan, king + wing, mug + rug, pen + ten, frog + dog, toy + boy

Page 140: Middle letter sounds

h<u>a</u>t, p<u>i</u>n, m<u>o</u>p, cr<u>i</u>b, b<u>a</u>t

Page 141: Consonant blends

<u>br</u>ead, <u>fr</u>og, <u>fl</u>y, <u>pl</u>ant, <u>cl</u>oud, <u>gl</u>ue, <u>cr</u>ab

Page 142: More blending

<u>cl</u>ick, <u>dr</u>ink, <u>st</u>airs, <u>cr</u>own, <u>sn</u>owman, <u>fl</u>ower, <u>gr</u>apes

Page 143: Ending blending

fi<u>sh</u>, du<u>ck</u>, te<u>nt</u>, ha<u>nd</u>, clo<u>ck</u>, sta<u>mp</u>, mi<u>lk</u>, la<u>mp</u>, a<u>nt</u>

Page 144: Is it 'ou' or 'oo'?

ou h<u>ou</u>se, m<u>ou</u>se

oo b<u>oo</u>k, m<u>oo</u>n

Page 145: Is it 'ou' or 'ow'?

ou m<u>ou</u>se, cl<u>ou</u>d, h<u>ou</u>se

ow cr<u>ow</u>n, cl<u>ow</u>n, fl<u>ow</u>er

Page 146: Is it 'oy' or 'oi'?

oy b<u>oy</u>, t<u>oy</u>

oi p<u>oi</u>nt, c<u>oi</u>n, f<u>oi</u>l, t<u>oi</u>let

Page 147: Is it 'ow' or 'oa'?

a. sn<u>ow</u>, b. arr<u>ow</u>, c. wind<u>ow</u>, d. g<u>oa</u>t, e. c<u>oa</u>t

Page 148: Is it 'ay' or 'ai'?

r<u>ai</u>n, st<u>ay</u>, w<u>ay</u>, d<u>ay</u>, tr<u>ai</u>n, p<u>ai</u>nt, w<u>ai</u>t, pl<u>ay</u>, tr<u>ay</u>

Page 149: The 'igh' combination

s<u>igh</u>, fr<u>igh</u>t, br<u>igh</u>t, n<u>igh</u>t, l<u>igh</u>tning, h<u>igh</u>, m<u>igh</u>t, s<u>igh</u>t

Page 150: Is it 'ar' or 'or'?

ar st<u>ar</u>, c<u>ar</u>, j<u>ar</u>

or c<u>or</u>n, f<u>or</u>k, th<u>or</u>n

Page 151: Is it 'air' or 'ir'?

air st<u>air</u>, f<u>air</u>, ecl<u>air</u>, ch<u>air</u>

ir b<u>ir</u>d, g<u>ir</u>l

Page 153: Wordsearch

d	e	v	z	l	m	a	r	k	p
a	s	d	f	s	p	o	o	n	g
h	p	a	r	t	j	k	b	x	l
z	x	c	v	a	b	n	m	q	a
w	s	c	t	r	e	e	d	c	r
f	v	t	g	b	y	h	n	u	b
j	m	i	h	k	m	e	e	t	e
o	l	z	o	p	o	q	l	w	a
a	s	j	o	w	o	g	i	d	k
s	e	a	t	b	n	f	h	q	a

Page 154: Which spelling?

A small animal with a long tail is called a **mouse.**

A man who wears a crown and lives in a palace is called a **king.**

When you don't wash your hands, they get **dirty.**

An animal with a long trunk is called an **elephant.**

When you are walking in the woods, you must follow the **path.**

Someone who lives on a farm is a **farmer.**

Page 156: You're the teacher!

a. The nurse was very <u>noisy</u>.

b. Correct.

c. Once upon a time there was a <u>princess</u>.

d. Five <u>years</u> ago, we moved to Maryland.

e. <u>When</u> will it be time to go home?

Page 158: More nonsense words

vurk, kear, thorden, queck, jigh, zurd, nud, plab, flurp